Property of

Presented to

_____

by

_____

on

_____

God's Story for Me

Bible Storybook

104 Favorite Bible Stories for Children

Published by Gospel Light
Ventura, California, U.S.A.
www.gospellight.com

Library of Congress Cataloging-in-Publication Data

God's story for me : 104 favorite Bible stories for children /
illustrated by Cheryl Nobens.
    p. cm.
 ISBN 978-0-8307-4812-9 (hard cover)
 1. Bible stories, English. I. Nobens, C. A.
 BS551.3.G64 2009
 220.9'505--dc22
                            2009011217

Rights for publishing this book outside the U.S.A. or in non-English languages are
administered by Gospel Light Worldwide, an international not-for-profit ministry.
For additional information, please visit www.glww.org, email info@glww.org, or
write to Gospel Light Worldwide, 1957 Eastman Avenue, Ventura, CA 93003, U.S.A.

Printed in China

Dear Parents,

God has a story to tell you and your child. It's the one true love story from which which all other love stories flow. **God's Story for Me** is the Bible storybook designed to write this never-ending love story forever in the hearts and lives of your child.

You and your child will enjoy

- reading this storybook at bedtime or family time

- getting into the action of each story through the colorful illustrations

- talking about the meaning of each story as you use each story's Connection Circle

- personalizing the storybook with cool stickers

So as you look at the pictures, read each story told in words your child will understand and connect the story to your child's life, you'll be leading your child to faith in Jesus.

God's Story for Me
104 Favorite Bible Stories for Children

Old Testament Stories

New Testament Stories

The Old Testament

God Makes the Earth

Genesis 1:1-19

In the beginning, there were no tall trees. There were no flowers, no animals or people! There was only DARKNESS. But God was there. And this is what God did.

First, God said, "Let there be LIGHT!" And just
like that, there was light! God called the light
"day." God also made the quiet dark time. He
called it "night."

Next, God made the sky—high and blue. God
made fluffy white clouds. They floated in the
wide, blue sky.

God put some water here and some there.
Rivers and lakes flowed into oceans. God made
big mountains and small hills. The land kept
the waters apart.

Then God said, "Trees, grass—grow! Fruit and flowers—grow!" And they did! Tall trees and soft green grass, fruit trees and vegetable plants, tiny flowers and berry bushes all began to grow.

God made the world to show His power and His love for us.

But God was not finished!

God made special lights in the sky. God made the sun to shine in the daytime. He made the moon. It glows in the night. God made every star that twinkles in the sky.

God Makes Animals

Genesis 1:20-25

God's world was full of mountains and trees. It had oceans and lakes. But it was very still. No fish swam in the water. No birds flew in the sky. It was quiet.

God said, "Let the water be filled with living things!" WOW! Little shiny fish wiggled and scooted. Red and blue and yellow fish swam fast. Sea horses bobbed, whales flipped their tails. Dolphins jumped and swam.

God said, "Let there be birds—birds of all kinds!" And big eagles spread their wings wide. Birds of every color swooped and sang.

Chickens flapped their wings
and clucked. Ducks dipped
their heads and quacked. But
God wasn't finished!

God said, "Let there be animals on the land!"
And horses ran in the fields. Cows mooed and
chewed. Cats meowed and chased squeaky mice.
Bears growled. Lions and tigers roared.

God made amazing animals. He gave us a wonderful place to live.

Now lively animals were everywhere!
God looked at the waters full of fish.
He looked at the skies filled with birds.
He looked at the land full of animals.
God said that it was very good.

God Makes People

Genesis 1:26-31; 2:7-23; 3:20

God saw the whole world He had made. He saw sky, hills, water and trees. He saw the sun and moon. God's world was beautiful!

God was glad to see the fish and birds, lizards and furry animals He had made. But God was not finished!

God made a man. God named the man
Adam. God told Adam, "I have a job for
you to do. Please name all of the animals."

But God still was not finished! He said, "It isn't good for Adam to be alone. I'll make a person who's perfect for him to love." So God made a woman. Adam named her Eve.

God made people so that He could love us and we could love Him.

God loved Adam and Eve. He told them, "Take care of the animals and birds and everything you see in My world."

God's creation was finished! And it was all very good!

God Loves Adam and Eve

Genesis 2:16-17; 3

God put Adam and Eve in a beautiful garden. They were glad to take care of the garden. They loved God, and God loved them.

The garden had many trees in it. But God showed Adam one special tree. God said, "You may eat from ALL the other trees But DO NOT eat this fruit."

One day, a snake came to the garden. The snake was really God's enemy, Satan. Satan told Eve, "You can eat the fruit from the special tree."

Eve listened to Satan. She looked at the fruit on that tree. She picked it. She bit into it. She gave some to Adam. Adam ate it, too.

As soon as Adam and Eve ate that fruit, they knew they had done wrong. They felt sad. They ran away and hid. God called, "Adam, where are you?" Adam said, "I was hiding. I was afraid."

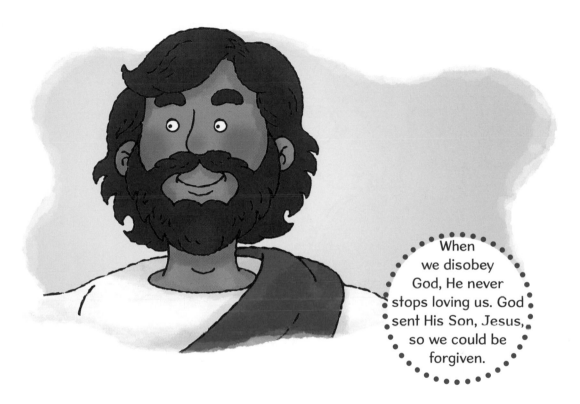

When we disobey God, He never stops loving us. God sent His Son, Jesus, so we could be forgiven.

Adam and Eve had disobeyed. God told them they must leave the garden. But God never stopped loving them. God gave them a happy promise: Someone would come to make things right again.

Noah Obeys God

Genesis 6:5—7:16

God made a beautiful world! But people stopped obeying God. They said mean things. They didn't care if they hurt each other.

God saw this. It made Him very sad. So God talked to a man named Noah.

God said, "I must send a flood. Rain will fall. Water will cover everything." "But your family will be safe. The animals will be safe, too." "Build a boat, just the way I tell you to build it."

Noah and his family listened and obeyed! They chopped trees and cut wood. They pounded boards and brushed on tar.

They worked hard for a long time. They did
everything God said to do. Finally, the big boat
was finished.

Then Noah's family loaded food onto the boat. They carried bundles and baskets up the ramp. Now there was food for hungry animals and hungry people! God said, "Bring the animals into the boat."

Obeying God helps us stay away from trouble. Obeying shows we love God.

Bears thumped up the ramp.
Birds flew through the door.
Rabbits hopped. Elephants bumped. At last,
every kind of animal was safe in the big boat.
Noah, his wife and his family came aboard, too.
Then God closed the door.

The Great Flood

Genesis 7:1—9:17

For 40 days, it rained and RAINED. The big boat bobbed on the water. Noah's family worked hard. They had to feed the animals. Would they float forever? No.

One day, the rain stopped. No more dripping.
Then BUMP! The boat landed. The water went
down a little every day.

Noah's family waited and waited. Finally
God said, "Come on out!" Noah's family swung
open the big door.

Big bears paused to sniff the air. Hippos, lambs and lizards ran outside! Birds flew away, higher and higher.

Noah and his family stood in the sun. They prayed and thanked God.

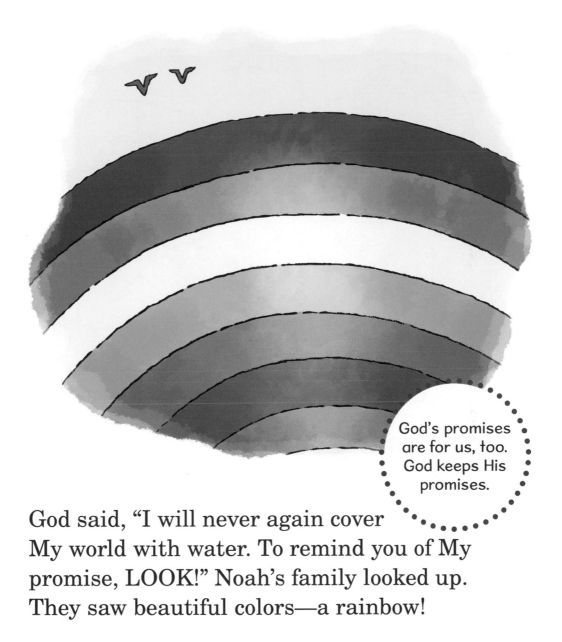

God said, "I will never again cover
My world with water. To remind you of My
promise, LOOK!" Noah's family looked up.
They saw beautiful colors—a rainbow!

Abraham Moves to a New Land

Genesis 12:1-8

God told Abraham, "I want you to move to a new land. I will show you how to get there."

Abraham told his wife, Sarah. "We are going to move."

So the family packed food and clothes.
They packed tents and blankets. They tied
bundles and baskets to camels and donkeys.
They brought along sheep and goats.

Every day, they walked.
God told them just where to go.
Every night, they put up tents.
They ate and slept. They walked
and walked.

God is always with us. He helps us everywhere we go.

One day, God told Abraham, "This is the place! It will be your new home." Abraham and his family thanked God. He had led them safely to a new land!

Abraham Shares

Genesis 13

Abraham lived near his nephew Lot. Each of them had herds of sheep, dozens of donkeys and lots of goats and cows.

There was not enough grass and water for SO
many animals. So Abraham's helpers argued
with Lot's helpers! "This is OUR water!" said
one. "No! This is OURS!" said another.

Abraham told Lot, "Let's not fight. Let's give our animals more room to eat and drink!" Abraham and Lot climbed a hill to see all the land. Abraham said, "Lot, you choose. Take whatever land you want." Lot chose the flat, grassy land. He and his animals moved away.

God gives us everything we need. We can be kind and share.

Abraham lived in a hilly land. There was not as much grass. But Abraham knew God would take care of him—and all of his animals!

Isaac Is Born

Genesis 17:15-19; 18:1-15; 21:1-8

Abraham and Sarah were very old. But God promised them a son. Abraham laughed when he heard this news. He thought they were too old to have a baby.

One day, three men came to visit Abraham and
Sarah. One visitor was God! He told Abraham
again,"You will have a son!"

Now Sarah laughed—how could this be? But
God said, "NOTHING is too hard for Me! Next
year, you WILL have a son!"

All of God's promises will come true. God never lies.

Just as God promised, Isaac was born!

God Helps Eliezer

Genesis 24

Abraham was very, very old. Now baby Isaac was all grown up! Abraham wanted Isaac to get married. So he asked his helper Eliezer, "Please, find a wife for Isaac. Go to the town where my relatives live. God will help you."

Eliezer packed his bundles on camels. Eliezer
wondered, *How can I find the right woman?*
He prayed, "God, please help me find the right
wife for Isaac. Have her give me a drink—and
then water my camels, too."

Eliezer came to the town. At the well, a beautiful young lady was getting water. Eliezer asked her for a drink. She gave him a drink. Then she said, "I'll water your camels, too."

Eliezer knew that this was the woman God had chosen! Her name was Rebekah. She brought Eliezer to her house. He asked if Rebekah would marry Isaac. Rebekah said YES!

So, Eliezer and Rebekah rode camels back to where Abraham and Isaac lived.

We can talk to God any time. God hears our prayers.

Isaac was glad to meet Rebekah!
He loved her. He married her.

Jacob and Esau

Genesis 25:19-28

Isaac and Rebekah had no children. So Isaac prayed. God answered Isaac's prayer!

Soon, their baby would be born. While they waited, God told Rebekah, "You'll give birth to two babies." Rebekah and Isaac would have twins!

The twins were born at last—two boys.

One boy was very red with lots of hair. His parents named him Esau. The other boy was named Jacob.

The boys grew older. They still were very different. Esau liked to hunt for animals. Isaac loved
Esau the hunter.

Each boy and girl is special and unique. There is no one else just like you!

Jacob liked to be at home and cook good food. Rebekah loved Jacob the helper. Isaac and Rebekah were glad. God gave them TWO sons to love!

An Unfair Trade

Genesis 25:27-34

Esau and Jacob were Isaac's twin sons.
Esau was born first. He had the birth-
right: He would become the family's leader.
He would get more of his father's things.

Jacob was younger. He would NOT be the
leader. He would get less from his father.

One day, Esau had been out hunting. He came home very hungry! He smelled Jacob's good stew. "Give me some stew!" he said.

"You want my stew?" asked Jacob. "Then trade me your birthright for this bowl of stew." Jacob wanted to be the family leader.

God wants us to make good choices and be kind to our family.

"I'll DIE if I don't eat," said Esau. "My birthright won't matter then. So—fine! You can HAVE my birthright. Now, give me that stew!" So Esau traded his important birthright. He traded it for a bowl of stew! The trade was not fair.

Isaac Digs Wells

Genesis 26:12-33

God helped Isaac grow lots of food. Isaac had many animals, too. Now, plants and animals need water! So Isaac's helpers dug some wells—deep holes that filled with water.

But Isaac's neighbors said, "This water is OURS!" Isaac did not fight with his neighbors. Instead, he moved away. So the neighbors got the water.

Isaac's helpers dug new wells. Then the neighbors came to argue. They wanted that water, too. So Isaac did not argue. He moved again and dug another well.

Now there was more water. But would the neighbors come to argue again? God told Isaac, "Don't be afraid. I am with you. I will help you."

Soon, the neighbors did visit again! Did they want to argue? No! They said, "God is helping you. We won't take your water. Let's be friends."

So Isaac was glad. He made a big dinner for the neighbors. Everyone was happy!

Jacob's Tricks

Genesis 27:1-45

Now Isaac was old. He was blind, too. He said, "Before I die, I want to give Esau my blessing. He is my older son. He will be our leader when I die."

Remember, Jacob had Esau's birthright. He would be the family leader. But Jacob wanted to get Esau's blessing, too. He didn't care about telling the truth!

So Rebekah and Jacob made a plan. They wanted to trick Isaac. Rebekah put goatskins on Jacob's arms. The skins made his arms feel hairy. Jacob put on Esau's coat. Now he smelled and felt like Esau!

Dressed as Esau, Jacob took food to Isaac. Isaac asked, "Are you REALLY Esau? You feel and smell like Esau. But you sound like Jacob!"

Jacob lied to his father. He said, "No, no! I'm Esau!" So Isaac gave Jacob the blessing. Jacob got the blessing meant for Esau.

God wants us to be honest and to tell the truth.

Then Esau came home. Jacob had stolen his blessing. Esau wanted to hurt Jacob!

Jacob was afraid. So he ran far, far from home. He was gone for many years.

Esau Forgives

Genesis 32:3-21; 33:1-11

Jacob stayed FAR away from Esau for years.
But one day God told Jacob, "It's time for you
to go home." So Jacob's family, animals and
helpers all began walking home.

When they were close to home, some of Jacob's helpers ran to tell him, "Esau and 400 men are coming this way!" Jacob was afraid. Was Esau still angry?

Jacob prayed, "Please keep us safe!" Then he decided, *I'll send Esau gifts! Maybe then he won't be angry.*

Jacob sent flocks of goats and sheep and camels,
herds of cows and donkeys—lots of animals!
Jacob walked far ahead, bowing.

Jacob looked up. Esau was running. Oh, no!
Was Esau going to hurt him?

No! Esau forgave Jacob. They hugged! Jacob
wasn't afraid any more. The brothers were
together again!

God Is with Joseph

Genesis 37; 39

Jacob had 12 sons. But Jacob loved his son Joseph best. Jacob gave Joseph a beautiful coat. That coat made his brothers angry!

Later Joseph had two dreams. He told his family, "In the dreams, you bowed to me." This made his brothers very angry!

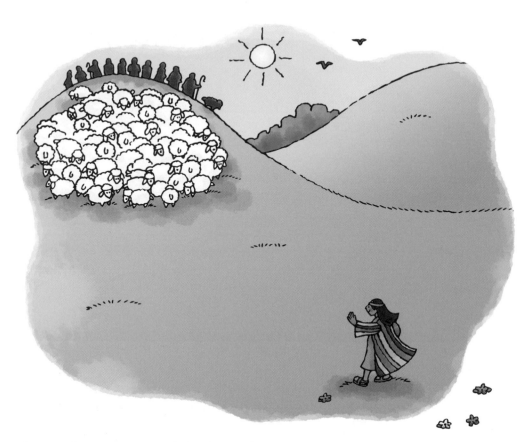

One day, Joseph's brothers took the family's
sheep to find new grass. They were gone for a
long time! Jacob sent Joseph to find them. Joseph walked and walked and walked. Joseph's
brothers saw him coming. They were still angry.
They wanted to hurt Joseph!

The brothers took Joseph's coat. They threw
Joseph into a deep hole. Then they saw some
traders coming. One brother said, "Let's sell
Joseph to them. They will take him far, far
away." So they sold Joseph to the traders.

Even when things are hard or we are hurt, God will never leave us.

Joseph was taken far away to Egypt. He was sold to be a worker. He did good work! God helped him. Then someone told lies about him. Joseph was put in the king's jail! But Joseph knew God was with him.

Joseph Rules

Genesis 41:1—42:8; 43:16; 45; 46:5-7

Joseph hadn't done anything wrong. But someone lied about him and he was put in jail! Two
men in jail had strange dreams. God helped
Joseph know what these dreams meant.

One of those men was let out of jail. He went
back to work for the king of Egypt. Then the
king had a strange dream. The man Joseph
had helped in jail told the king about Joseph.
The king said, "Bring Joseph to me!"

Joseph went to listen to the king. The king told
Joseph his strange dream. Joseph said, "God has
helped me to know this: In seven years, food will
not grow. Save extra grain now. We can eat the
grain we save during this time when no food
grows."

The king of Egypt said, "God did help you! You'll be in charge of saving grain!"

So Joseph became a ruler in Egypt. His helpers built big barns. Extra grain was put into the barns. For seven years, they saved grain. When NO grain grew, Egypt had food!

Joseph's own family needed food, too. Jacob heard Egypt had grain. He told his sons, "Go! Buy grain for us."

Ten brothers traveled to Egypt. They bowed low to ask for grain. They didn't know they bowed to Joseph—he looked like a king! Joseph sold them grain and they left.

But soon, they needed more grain! The brothers
came back and bowed. This time Joseph said,
"Look! It's ME! Joseph!" The brothers were afraid.
They had been so mean to Joseph. Would he be
mean to them?

God makes good things happen when we obey Him. We can obey in good and bad times.

No! Joseph forgave them! "You meant to hurt me," he said, "but God meant to help! HE put me here! Bring our father Jacob and your families here to live!" ALL of Joseph's family moved to Egypt. They were together again!

God Protects Moses

Exodus 1:8—2:10

God's people lived in a country where there was a MEAN king. This mean king made everyone work very hard. Even worse, he wanted to get rid of ALL the boy babies!

One family had a baby named Moses. They
loved Moses. They wanted to keep him safe!

So God gave Moses' mom an idea. She made a
special basket that could float. Then she put
Moses in the basket.

She carried the basket to the river. She floated
it on the water. Moses' big sister Miriam stayed
to watch Moses.

Soon the mean king's daughter, the princess, came to the river. She saw the basket. She opened the basket. There was a baby boy! Miriam was brave. She asked, "Shall I find someone to take care of this baby?" "Yes!" said the princess.

God gives us people who care for us, even in scary times.

Miriam RAN to get her mom! SHE could take good care of Moses! Moses' family was glad that baby Moses was safe.

God's People Escape

Exodus 3:1—12:38; 13:20-22

Moses was a grown-up now. God told him, "I have chosen you to be the leader of My people. Lead them to the land I promised to give them."

So Moses went to the mean king. Moses told
him what God said. The mean king said, "NO!"
No one will leave Egypt!"

So God made sure that the king would
change his mind! He sent millions of flies
and frogs. Grasshoppers came and ate
up the plants! Animals and people
got sick and died.

The mean king finally changed his mind. He said, "Leave! ALL of you!"

The people bundled up tents and blankets.
They gathered things they needed. And so God's
people escaped from Egypt.

Moses told the people, "God will lead us. He will
show us where to go and take care of us."

In the daytime, God led them with a big white
cloud. The cloud made shade in the hot desert.
God's people followed the cloud.

At night, God led them with a tall
fire in the sky. God's fire gave them
light and warmth. They knew where to go.
They knew God was with them.

God takes
care of us. He
teaches us the
right way
to live.

God's Path Through the Sea

Exodus 14:1—15:2

God's people walked and walked! They followed
God's big cloud and fire. They camped beside a
big sea. But far off, they saw dust rising. The
mean king's army was coming to take them
back to Egypt!

God told Moses, "I will help you. The mean king's army won't get you." God moved His big cloud. God's people were hidden by the cloud! Then Moses said, "Let's cross the sea. God told me what to do." Moses raised his hand. Strong winds blew until the sea became dry land!

The water piled up high on either side! The people and animals walked across! When everyone was safely across, Moses raised his hand again. The waters came together—CRASH! SPLASH!

We can sing and dance and celebrate because God loves us and cares for us.

The people sang and thanked God. They danced for joy! God kept His people safe!

God Gives Food and Water

Exodus 15:22-25; 16

God's people had walked for three days. They had not seen any water. They were thirsty! When they finally saw water, they hurried to take a drink. Oh, no! The water tasted bad!

So Moses prayed and God helped. God showed
Moses a piece of wood. Moses threw it into
the water. Then the water tasted good! So the
people drank and splashed!

But now everyone grew hungry! And there was
no food! So Moses prayed and God helped.

We can pray and ask God for what we need. He will help us.

God sent small birds into the camp. The people could eat the meat! The next morning little round things lay all over the ground. "What IS it?" asked the people. Moses told them, "God gave you bread. Take all you need for today!" God gave His people water and food!

God Gives His Law

Exodus 19:1—20:17

God's people walked and walked. They walked to big Mount Sinai. They camped near the tall mountain. Moses went UP the mountain! He went to listen to God.

God told Moses, "I have cared for you and helped you. I want these people to be My people. Tell
the people to get ready. I am going to give you
My laws. Then you'll know the best way to live."

The people got ready. Then, God sent lightning and thunder. There was smoke. The earth shook! God had come to give them His laws.

God said, "Love and worship only Me. Do not make statues to bow down to. Use My name in good ways.

God loves us. When we obey His rules, we know the best way to live.

"Love and obey your parents. Don't hurt other people. Don't take what is not yours. Say only true words. Be glad for what you have." God's ten commandments are His rules for us to follow.

Exploring the Promised Land

Numbers 13:1—14:35

God's people were close to the new land God had promised them. So Moses chose 12 men. They went to explore the new land.

The new land was beautiful! Good food grew in
that land! The 12 men also saw people—very
big people! They returned to their camp.

TEN of the men were very scared. They said,
"The people are too strong. We're like grasshoppers beside them!" But Caleb and Joshua said,
"Don't be afraid. God is with us! He wants us to
go into the land."

No one listened to Caleb and Joshua. But they
did listen to the 10 men. Soon everyone was
afraid and crying! God told Moses, "Because
these people do not trust Me, they will not go
into the Promised Land."

For 40 more years, God's people walked around in the desert.

We can trust God and know He will take care of us. God has good things for us.

Finally, all the people who had not trusted God were gone. But Caleb and Joshua were still alive. God had told them, "Because you trusted Me, you'll live in the Promised Land."

Crossing the River

Joshua 3—4

God's people were camped by the Jordan River. Across the river, they could see the land God had promised them!

But the water in the river was deep. It was fast. It was scary! There were no boats and no bridges. And no one could swim across that fast river! How would they get across? Joshua, their leader, told them, "God will do an amazing thing!" So the people packed up to go.

Joshua told everyone, "Walk behind the Ark* of the Lord!" Chosen men carried the Ark. When their toes touched the river, God stopped the water! Far upriver, it stood like a wall!

* The Ark was a beautiful golden box. It showed the people that God was with them.

The men who held the Ark stood in the middle
of the riverbed. After everyone walked across,
12 family leaders went back. Each one picked
up a big river stone.

Finally, everyone was safe and in their land!
Then God told Joshua, "Tell the men carrying
the Ark to walk out of the Jordan." WHOOSH!
The water filled the river again!

When we're afraid, God's power can help us. We can tell others about God's power.

The 12 men piled the river stones into a tall pile. These stones would remind them to tell what amazing things God did!

Walls Fall Down

Joshua 6

God's people were in their new land! But people lived there already. They did not want to share this land!

Some of these people lived in Jericho. It was a city with very big walls! But God told His plan to Joshua: "March your army around Jericho. For six days, march one time each day.

"On the seventh day, march around SEVEN times. Have the priests blow the horns. Then they will blow long and loud. Tell the people, 'When you hear that long, loud trumpet sound, SHOUT! The walls of the city will fall down!'"

Joshua told the people God's plan. The big walls looked very strong! But God's people obeyed. On day one, they marched. All around Jericho's tall walls, they marched. No one said a word. Silently, they went back to their camp. For five more days, they did this.

But the seventh day came. They marched
around seven times! The priests blew their
horns. Then they blew long and loud. Everyone SHOUTED!

Sometimes God's plans are different from how we would do things. God's plans are good.

The ground began to shake. The walls began to crack! The walls crumbled and CRASHED! And God's people marched straight into the city, just as God had promised!

Deborah Helps God's People

Judges 4:1-16; 5:4,20-21

God's people were NOT obeying God. And big trouble was on its way: An army was coming to fight them! This army had many strong chariots! So God's people finally asked God for help.

God told a leader named Deborah, "Tell Barak the army general that I say, 'Get lots of men. I will help you defeat that big army.'"

But Barak was afraid! He said, "Deborah, I will go IF you go with me. If you don't go, I won't go." Deborah told him, "I will go with you."

Barak asked God's people to help. Soon lots of men came together. They all climbed Mount Tabor. From the mountain, they could see nine hundred chariots rolling across the flat land. The chariots came closer and closer.

Deborah told Barak, "Go! God will help you. You will win!" Barak did what Deborah said, and just like that, God won the battle!

When the battle was over, Deborah and Barak sang. They sang about the way God won the battle! Everyone praised God!

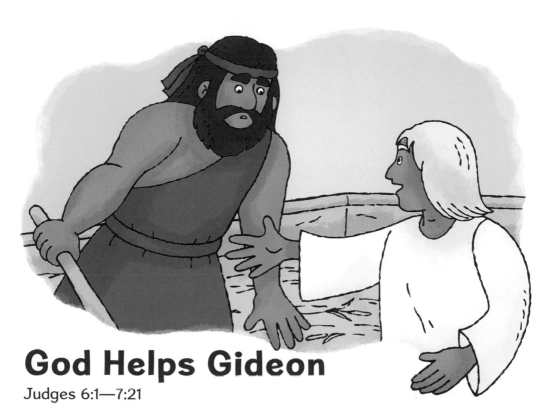

God Helps Gideon

Judges 6:1—7:21

God's people were not obeying God. And now they were in trouble: The Midianites were stealing their food! God's people were hiding because of their fear. They finally asked God for His help!

God sent an angel to Gideon. The angel said, "God wants to help you get the Midianites out of Israel."

At first, Gideon was scared. He asked God to show His power by making some fleece wet, and then dry. God did! Then Gideon bravely obeyed God!

Gideon gathered men to be soldiers. But God said there were too many. So Gideon said, "If you are scared, you may go home!" Many men went home!

Then God told Gideon, "There are still too many men." God wanted Gideon to know that GOD would win the battle, not soldiers! So Gideon sent even more men home.

Then God told Gideon just what to do. He gave
everyone a trumpet, a jar and a torch. The men
circled the Midianite camp. In the dark, they lit
the torches. They covered them with the jars.
Then at Gideon's signal, everyone broke the
jars, blew the trumpets and shouted!

God cares for us. He will help us know what to do when people are mean to us.

The Midianites heard the noise. They saw the lights—and ran! Gideon and his men chased them away. GOD saved His people, just as He promised. God did not need a big army!

Ruth Is Faithful

Ruth 1—4

Ruth and Naomi were alone. They had no food.
They had no money to buy food.

So Ruth and Naomi walked and walked. They came to Bethlehem. It was Naomi's hometown. At that time, the barley was ripe.

Ruth went to a barley field. She walked after the harvest workers. She picked up the barley they left.

She took it home to share with Naomi. Now they had food! Ruth was glad to help Naomi.

Someone had noticed Ruth working. His name
was Boaz. He owned the field where Ruth
worked. He saw how kind Ruth was. He gave
Ruth extra barley. He said, "Please, stay in my
field. Drink water from my water jars."

God wants us to care about others and work hard to help them.

Boaz helped Ruth and Naomi. He helped Naomi get her land back. Then Boaz and Ruth got married! Then they had a baby named Obed*. Naomi was so happy!

* Obed grew up. His son was Jesse. Then Jesse had a son named David. David became Israel's great king!

God Hears Hannah

1 Samuel 1; 2:11,18-21,26

Hannah had no children—not one. That made her very sad!

Every year, Hannah and her husband worshiped God at the Tabernacle. The Tabernacle was the big tent where God's people prayed to God.

One day, Hannah whispered to God, "Please give me a son. I'll teach him to love and obey You. Please, give me a baby!"

Eli the teacher saw Hannah. He said, "I'll ask God to give what you've asked." Hannah went home very happy! She knew God listens.

Months later, baby Samuel was born! Hannah
took good care of him! Then Samuel grew older.
Hannah took him to the Tabernacle.

Samuel lived and worked there with Eli. And
every year, Hannah visited him. She always
brought Samuel a new coat. She made it just
for him!

God wants us to talk to Him. Talking and listening to God is one way we love Him.

Samuel grew and learned. He listened to and obeyed God!

Samuel Listens to God

1 Samuel 3

One night, Samuel was asleep. But he heard something—a voice! The voice was calling, "Samuel!"

Samuel got right up and ran to Eli. "Here I am, Eli! Did you call me?"

Eli said, "I didn't call you, Samuel." So Samuel ran back and got into bed. But he heard that voice again! He ran to Eli again! But Eli said, "I did not call you, Samuel!"

By now, Samuel was wide awake! He heard that voice AGAIN—"Samuel!"

Samuel got right up. He ran to Eli. "Here I am, Eli! Did you call me?" Samuel asked.

Eli said, "If you hear that voice again, say this: 'Speak, Lord. I'm listening.'"

"All right!" said Samuel.

God is happy when we obey Him. We can learn how to obey God by listening to His Word.

NOW that voice called his name again! "Samuel! Samuel!"

"Speak, Lord. I'm listening!" he said. Eli was right! God had been calling! Samuel listened carefully. He did his best to remember every word God had to say! As he grew up, Samuel listened to God—and obeyed!

God Chooses David

1 Samuel 16:1-13

God told Samuel, "I have decided that King Saul won't be king much longer. One of Jesse's sons will be Israel's king. Go to Jesse's house. Anoint* this new king."

* "Anoint" means to put a little oil on a person to show God has chosen him or her.

So Samuel traveled to Jesse's house. Jesse
called his sons together. Samuel met the oldest
who was tall and strong. But Samuel shook his
head no. He was NOT the one God had chosen.

Samuel met six more sons. But Samuel kept shaking his head no. Samuel asked, "Are there any more?"

Jesse said, "One more son is out taking care of the sheep." Samuel asked to meet him.

No matter how old or young we are, loving God is what's most important.

The youngest son came. His name was David. "THIS is the one!" God told Samuel. God knew that David loved Him. So Samuel put oil on David's head. God had chosen David to be Israel's new king!

The Lord Is My Shepherd

Psalm 23

David wrote a song about how God loves us and cares for us like a shepherd cares for his sheep.

"God is my shepherd. He gives me everything
   I need.
He gives me good food and water.
He shows me the right way to go.

We can sing and thank God for His great love for us.

"Even when I'm scared, I know He is with me
and is taking care of me.
God fills my life with good things, and I know
I'll live forever with Him."

David the Hero

1 Samuel 17

David's seven big brothers joined King Saul's army. The army was fighting the Philistines. The BIGGEST Philistine was Goliath.

Every day, Goliath stood in the valley. He'd
yell: "Send someone to FIGHT me! If anyone
can knock me down, we Philistines will work for
YOU!" But NO one wanted to fight Goliath!
Everyone was afraid of him.

Meanwhile, Jesse told David, "Visit your brothers. Tell me if they are well. Pack up the donkeys with grain and cheese and bread to give them."

David walked and walked. Finally David saw the camp. He gave his brothers the food.

But while David was there, he heard Goliath shout! David asked, "Why doesn't someone fight him?" But everyone was afraid. "I'LL fight him!" David said. "GOD will help me!"

"I don't need armor," said David. He picked up five smooth little rocks. He put one in his sling-shot. He said to Goliath, "You have a sword. But I have GOD'S help!" David twirled the stone in his sling. It went around and around very fast.

The rock hit Goliath's head. Big
Goliath fell down—THUNK! God
had helped David win the battle! Everyone said
David was a hero!

God helps us
do big jobs. He is
stronger than
anything or
anyone!

David and Jonathan

1 Samuel 16:15-23; 18:1-4; 19:1-7

King Saul was VERY unhappy. But when David played his harp, King Saul felt better. So David came to live at the palace.

Jonathan was King Saul's son. Jonathan and
David became friends.

Jonathan and David promised to ALWAYS be best friends! Jonathan gave David his own coat. He gave David his own bow and arrow.

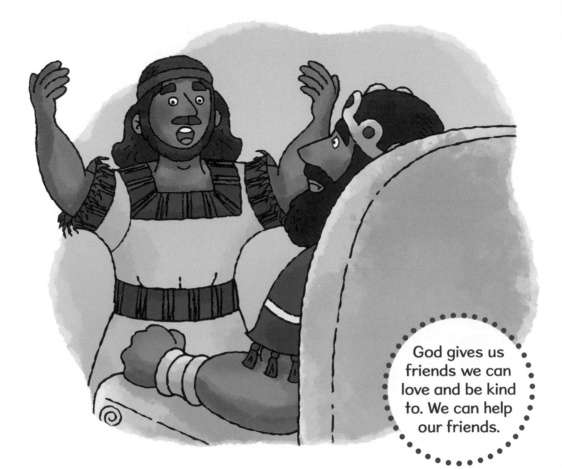

God gives us friends we can love and be kind to. We can help our friends.

Later on, King Saul was jealous of David and wanted to hurt him! Jonathan helped David hide. Then Jonathan talked with King Saul so that David could come back and be safe. The friends were glad to be together again!

David Is Kind to Saul

1 Samuel 26

King Saul did NOT want David to be king. He wanted to get rid of David. So David ran away and hid with his friends.

But King Saul's army looked for them. One
night, King Saul and his army were asleep.
David and a friend tiptoed to Saul. David's
friend wanted to hurt King Saul. But David
said, "NO! I won't hurt him!"

David and his friend took Saul's spear. They
took the water jug by his head. They carried
Saul's things to the top of a hill.

Then David shouted, "King Saul! Where is your water jug? Where is your spear?"

King Saul jumped up. He called back, "Is that you, David?"

Even when others are not kind to us, God will help us be kind to them.

David said, "I could have hurt you! But I did not."

King Saul said, "I was wrong. I won't try to hurt you. May God take care of you."

David Helps Mephibosheth

1 Samuel 20:14-17,42; 2 Samuel 9

David and Jonathan were best friends. They promised to help each other. They also promised to always take care each other's family.

Many years later, David was king. Jonathan
had died, but David did not forget him—or his
promise, either. He asked Ziba, "Is anyone still
alive from Jonathan's family? I want to be kind
and help!" Ziba told him about Mephibosheth.

Mephibosheth was one of Jonathan's sons. His feet were hurt. He didn't walk well. David sent servants to tell Mephibosheth that David wanted to see him.

Mephibosheth came to David's palace. David said, "Mephibosheth, don't be afraid. I want you to live here."

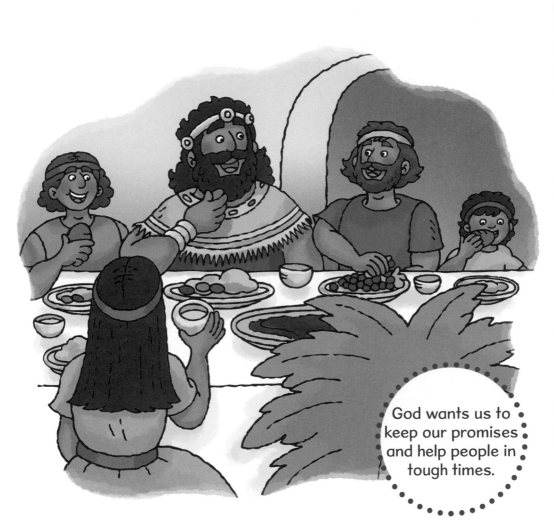

God wants us to keep our promises and help people in tough times.

David said, "I want you to eat with me. I will treat you like my own son." So Mephibosheth lived in the palace!

Solomon Becomes King

1 Kings 1:28-31; 3:1-13; 4:29-34; 6:1-14

King David chose his son Solomon to be king. King Solomon asked God to help him be wise. He asked God to help him be a good ruler.

God told Solomon, "You did not ask for money. You did not ask for long life. Since you asked to be a good king instead, I will give you wisdom. You will also be rich and have a long life!"

God made Solomon the wisest man EVER.
He also made Solomon the richest king! People
visited from all over the world. They wanted to
learn from wise Solomon.

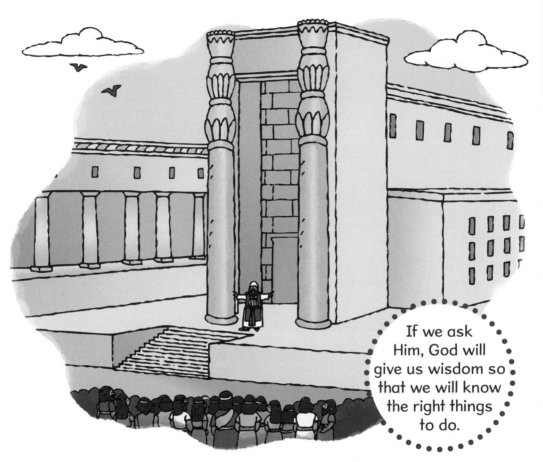

If we ask Him, God will give us wisdom so that we will know the right things to do.

Solomon built many wonderful buildings. The best building he built was a Temple for God. God's people went to the Temple to praise God. They prayed and worshiped God there. It was beautiful. And God was glad!

God Cares for Elijah

1 Kings 17:1-6

After Solomon was king, other kings ruled. Ahab was a very BAD king in Israel. He did not love and obey God. God sent Elijah the prophet to tell the king God's messages.

God told Elijah, "Go tell King Ahab there will be NO rain until you say so!" So Elijah told Ahab what God said. No rain meant everything would dry up. No food would grow. Everyone would be hungry!

King Ahab got very ANGRY! He wanted to hurt
Elijah!

God takes care of us every day. He knows what we need.

So God sent Elijah to hide in a safe place. Elijah lived beside a stream of water. Every day he drank water from this stream. Then God sent birds. They carried bread and meat to Elijah every day.

God Cares for a Widow

1 Kings 17:7-16

One day, the stream near Elijah dried up! So God told Elijah to go to a town. He said a woman there would have food. Elijah walked and walked and walked!

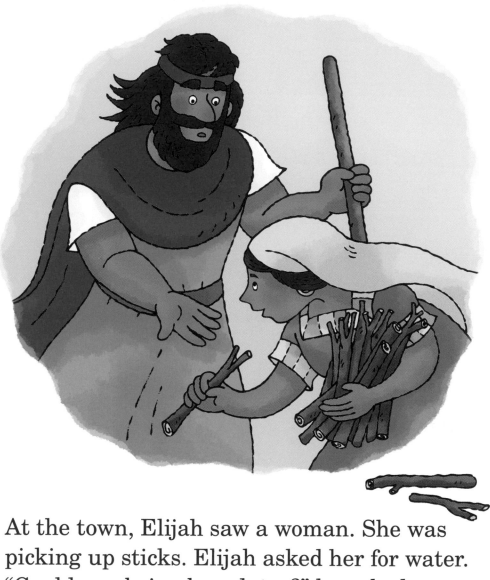

At the town, Elijah saw a woman. She was
picking up sticks. Elijah asked her for water.
"Could you bring bread, too?" he asked.

The woman said, "I have only enough flour and oil to make one last bit of bread for my son and me."

Elijah said, "Don't be afraid. Make a little bread for me first. God promised that there will be enough food for all of us!"

We can celebrate and thank God for all the good things He gives us.

So the woman baked bread for Elijah. Then she looked into her flour jar. There was more flour! She peeked into her oil pitcher. There was MORE oil! And every day after that, there was enough flour and oil.

Elijah and the Prophets of Baal

1 Kings 18:18-39

Elijah told King Ahab, "You have not obeyed God. You have worshiped the false god Baal. Tell the people and Baal's prophets to meet me on Mount Carmel."

On the big day, everyone came to the mountain.
Elijah said to the people, "Let us see who is
REALLY God. Baal's prophets will get a sacrifice ready. So will I. Then we'll pray. Whoever
answers the prayer by sending fire is the one,
true God!"

The people said, "This is a good idea!" So Baal's prophets got a sacrifice ready. Then they prayed, shouted and stomped! They did this ALL DAY LONG. But Baal did not send any fire.

In the evening, Elijah got a sacrifice ready. He had men pour water over it—three times! Then Elijah prayed, "O Lord God, please show these people that YOU are the one, true God!"

WHOOOOOOSH! God's fire came down! It burned up everything!

God is alive and powerful. He loves us. God wants us to love Him.

The people bowed to the ground. They could see that Baal had no power. They shouted, "The LORD—HE is GOD! The LORD—HE is GOD!"

Elisha and the Oil

2 Kings 4:1-7

A sad woman asked God's prophet Elisha for help. She said, "My husband died. He owed money. If I don't pay the money back, my boys will be sold as slaves!"

Elisha asked, "What do you have?"

"Nothing—except a little oil!" she said.

Elisha told her what to do: "Ask your neighbors for jars. Take the jars into the house. Pour oil into each jar."

The woman did! She and her boys filled jar
after jar after jar with oil. The oil did NOT run
out! When she asked for another jar, her son
said, "There aren't ANY jars left!" EVERY jar
in the house was full of oil!

Sometimes we have very little. Even then, God will take care of us and help us.

The woman went to tell Elisha. He said, "Now, sell the oil. Pay back the money. Then you and your sons can live on the money that is left." God took care of this family in an amazing way!

God Heals Naaman

2 Kings 5:1-15

Naaman was an important army commander.
But he had leprosy—painful sores all over.

A servant girl in his house told Naaman's wife,
"Elisha can ask God to help Naaman!"

When Elisha heard that Naaman had come
to be made well, he sent a message: "Have
Naaman come to me."

So Naaman went to Elisha's house. Elisha's servant told Naaman, "Elisha says to wash in the Jordan River seven times. Then you will be well." At first, Naaman was angry. Washing in a river sounded like a silly idea! He started to walk away.

But Naaman's servant said, "If you had to pay money or do something hard, you would do it! Why not obey?"

God cares about us when we are hurt or sick. He will never leave us alone.

So Naaman walked to the river. He ducked under—1, 2, 3, 4, 5, 6, 7 times! Naaman came up and his sores were gone! Naaman said, "The God of Israel has made me well. He is the one, true God!"

Joash Repairs the Temple

2 Kings 12:1-15; 2 Chronicles 24:1-14

God's Temple once was beautiful. People came there to pray to God. But after many years, no one came. No one prayed or sang there to God. The Temple was broken, dirty and dusty!

Then seven-year old Joash became king. He loved
God! Little King Joash grew up. He wanted God's
people to love God. So King Joash planned to
make the Temple beautiful once more.

Joash told the Temple helpers to say, "Please help us make the Temple beautiful. Bring money to the big box." People gave their money. Soon, the big money box was full.

Helpers sawed and hammered. Helpers swept and made bowls and candlesticks out of gold. Now the Temple was beautiful again!

Josiah Obeys God

2 Chronicles 34:1—35:19

Many years later, God's people had forgotten
how to obey the Lord again. Josiah became
their king when he was only eight years old.

Josiah told his workers, "Let's make God's Temple clean!" So the workers cleaned and swept. They lifted and dusted—and look! They found a scroll of God's Word!

A servant brought the scroll to Josiah. He read
the words carefully. Then King Josiah sent out
this order: "Come to hear God's words. We must
learn how to obey God!"

Reading God's Word and obeying Him makes us glad!

The people came to listen to God's Word. King Josiah read every word out loud. He said, "I will obey what I have read." God's people said they would obey, too! They were glad to know HOW to obey God. So for days, they sang and worshiped Him!

Nehemiah Rebuilds the Walls

Nehemiah 1—2; 4:1-6; 6:15-16; 12:27,43

Nehemiah lived in Babylon. He was the king's special helper. But Nehemiah was from Jerusalem. Nehemiah heard that the walls in Jerusalem were broken down. Nehemiah felt very sad about this. So he prayed and prayed.

Then he asked the king of Babylon, "Let me go to rebuild Jerusalem's walls." The king said yes!

So Nehemiah traveled to Jerusalem. He saw the broken walls. He saw the burned gates. He met the people living there. Nehemiah said, "Let's all build the walls!"

God wants us to work together. We can share the work and help each other.

Every family went to work. Some families built gates. Some families put stones into the walls. It took a long time. But one day, the work was done! Nehemiah and the people thanked God!

Esther Trusts God

Esther 2—9

Esther was one of God's people. She lived
in Persia. Her parents died. So her cousin
Mordecai took care of her.

King Xerxes chose Esther to be his queen. Esther went to live in his palace! King Xerxes gave her clothes and jewels. Esther was beautiful.

But Xerxes had a helper named Haman. Haman wanted to kill all God's people! He tricked the king into making a law that God's people could be killed. When Esther heard about the law, she said, "I will ask the king to stop this law."

But anyone who came to Xerxes without being asked could be killed—even Esther! So Esther, Mordecai and all God's people prayed! Then Esther went to King Xerxes's room. King Xerxes invited her in. God answered the prayers. Esther was safe.

Later, Esther told King Xerxes, "Someone wants to KILL me—and my people, too! Please save my life!" "Who would do such a terrible thing?" the king asked. Esther said, "The man is HAMAN!"

So King Xerxes had Haman taken away. Then King Xerxes made a new law. God's people were saved!

Jeremiah Tells God's Words

Jeremiah 36

God's prophet Jeremiah told the people God's words. Jeremiah would say God's words out loud. His helper Baruch wrote the words on a scroll.

Baruch took the scroll to the Temple. He read
the words in a loud voice. Everyone could hear
God's words. They knew they had not obeyed
God's words. Some people told the king about
the scroll.

"Bring the scroll!" the king said. A servant read
the words out loud. Each time the king listened
to a part, he cut off a piece of the scroll. He
threw each piece into a fire!

But the king could not stop God's words. God told Jeremiah, "Get Baruch. Write down My words again." Jeremiah and Baruch wrote all of God's words again, on a new scroll! The people STILL did not obey God. But Baruch and Jeremiah obeyed.

Daniel Obeys God

Daniel 1

The king of Babylon marched to Jerusalem. He burned the city and broke the walls. He took many people back to Babylon.

Daniel and his three friends had to go to Babylon. The king's helper said, "You will learn to work for the king. You'll eat food only from the king's table." But God's people were not to eat those foods. Daniel and his friends wanted to obey GOD.

So Daniel asked the guard, "Please, try this test: For 10 days, give us vegetables and water. Then see how we are." For 10 days, they ate only vegetables. They drank only water.

Learning about God helps us make right choices, even when it's hard.

After 10 days, the guard looked at them. Daniel and his friends looked strong! So the guard let them eat the same food they had been eating during the 10 days. Daniel and his friends learned more and more.

The Fiery Furnace

Daniel 3

Daniel's three friends worked for the king. This king made a BIG golden statue. He also made a new rule: "When the music plays, bow and pray to this statue. If you do not, you will be thrown into a furnace and burned up!"

Soon, the music began to play. People bowed
and prayed to the statue. But Daniel's friends
did not bow. They would pray only to God!

When the king heard about the three friends, he said, "If you don't bow, you'll be thrown into the furnace. Who'll help you then?"

The friends said, "O King, our God can save us. But even if He does not, we won't bow!"

NOW the king was VERY angry! He had the
furnace heated even more. Soldiers tied up the
three friends. Then they threw them into the
hot furnace!

The king stood up. "LOOK!" he said. "Didn't we throw in three? Now there are four! They are not tied up!"

God had sent an angel into that furnace. The friends were safe! The king shouted for the friends to come out—and they did! The three friends were not burned at ALL.

Every day, we can pray to the one, true God.

The king praised the one, true God. He said, "No one may say anything bad about the God of these friends. Only the one, true God could help people in this way!"

Writing on the Wall

Daniel 5

King Belshazzar was king of Babylon. He did not love God, but he did love parties! At one big party, he and his friends drank from gold cups made for God's Temple. The king disobeyed God.

Suddenly, a big HAND appeared! The hand
wrote words on the wall! Everyone grew very
quiet. And King Belshazzar grew very AFRAID!

The hand disappeared. But the words stayed on the wall. No one knew what the words meant. The king was even more afraid! The queen told the king, "Daniel will know what the words mean. Call him!"

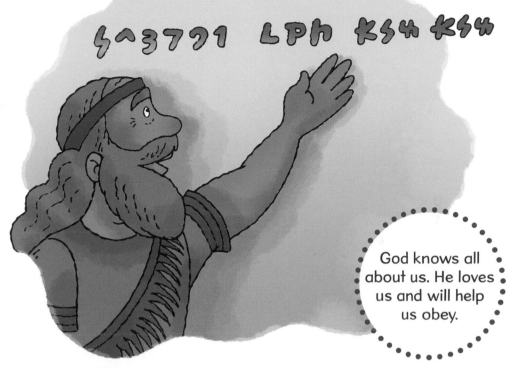

God knows all about us. He loves us and will help us obey.

Daniel came. He DID know. The words meant God knew that Belshazzar had disobeyed Him. His time as king was over. Another king would take his place.

It happened just as Daniel said it would. ANOTHER king took over that very night! Daniel became a helper of the new king.

The Lions' Den

Daniel 6

Daniel was a leader in Babylon. He did the best work of anyone! The other leaders didn't like this. They wanted to get rid of Daniel!

Everyone knew Daniel loved God. Three times a day, he went home to pray. So the other leaders made a new law. They got the king to agree: "You must pray to the KING or else you'll be thrown to the LIONS!"

But Daniel went home like he always did. He
knelt and prayed.

The other leaders soon told the king, "Daniel is praying to GOD, as always! He must be thrown into the lion's den!" The king was very upset. He saw he had been tricked. But he could not change the law.

So Daniel was put into the lions' den. All night, the king worried. In the morning, the king was up very early.

God is so powerful, He will always care for us.

"DANIEL!" he cried. "Did your God save you?"

Daniel said, "My God sent an angel. He shut those lions' mouths."

Now the king told everyone, "The one, true God kept Daniel safe!"

259

Jonah and the Big Fish

Jonah 1–4

Jonah told people messages from God. One day
God told him, "Go to Nineveh. Tell those people
to stop doing wrong." But Jonah did NOT like
those people! So he got onto a ship. It was going
away from Nineveh.

Down in the big ship, Jonah went to sleep. That's
when God sent a storm. The sailors were afraid.
But Jonah was asleep. The sailors shook Jonah
awake. "PLEASE PRAY!" they begged him.

Jonah knew God had sent the storm. So he said, "Throw me off the ship. Then the storm will stop." So one, two, THREE, they threw him off! SPLASH! Jonah sank deep into the water. And just like that, the storm stopped.

Suddenly, a HUGE fish swam by Jonah. It opened its mouth wide and WHOOSH! Jonah was in the big fish's belly! He asked God to forgive him. Jonah prayed and waited for three days.

The fish coughed out Jonah onto the sand.

When we do wrong, we can ask God to forgive us. And He will. He will never stop loving us.

God told Jonah again, "Tell the people in Nineveh what I say." Jonah obeyed this time! He talked and the people listened. They asked God to FORGIVE them. And God did.

The New Testament

John Is Born

Luke 1:5-25,57-80

Long ago, God promised to send a Savior. God sent angels to tell good news. God's promise would soon come true!

First, God sent an angel to Zechariah. He and his wife, Elizabeth, had no children. The angel said, "You will have a son! He will help people get ready for Jesus."

Zechariah didn't believe the angel. So the angel said, "You will be silent until the day my words come true." Zechariah was AMAZED. The angel was right. He could NOT talk! Zechariah went home. Soon Elizabeth was expecting a baby!

All the time, in the day and in the night, God will keep His promises to you.

Then Elizabeth's baby was born. His parents named him John. Suddenly, Zechariah could talk again. Zechariah told about wonderful things God was going to do when baby John grew up. He thanked God for keeping His promises!

Mary Hears Good News

Matthew 1:18-21; Luke 1:26-56

God sent an angel to tell Mary good news! The angel surprised her. The angel said, "Don't be afraid, Mary! God has important news for you. You will have a baby. Name Him Jesus. He is the Savior God promised to send—God's own Son."

Mary wanted to TELL her good news! She went to see her cousin, Elizabeth. Elizabeth would soon have a baby, too! Elizabeth also knew that Mary's baby would be the Savior God promised to send. Elizabeth and Mary praised God together!

God sent an angel to another person. Joseph was going to be Mary's husband. In a dream, an angel talked to him.

Jesus is the most special baby ever born. He is God's Son.

The angel said, "Don't be afraid to get married to Mary. The baby is the Savior God promised to send. Name the baby Jesus." Joseph believed God's promise was about to come true!

Jesus Is Born

Luke 2:1-7

Mary's baby would be born SOON. Joseph told Mary, "We must go to Bethlehem, my home-town. We must write our names in the king's tax book."

Mary and Joseph packed their things. Mary and Joseph walked and walked down the road to Bethlehem. At night, they stopped and slept. When morning came, they walked again!

Mary and Joseph got to Bethlehem at last.
The city was FULL of people. Joseph and
Mary needed a place to sleep. Joseph knocked
on the door of an inn. But there was no room.
It was full.

The innkeeper said, "Wait! You can use the stable!" Sheep, cows and donkeys slept there. But Joseph and Mary were glad for a place to rest!

That very night, in that very stable, Jesus was
born. Mary wrapped Him up safe and warm.

God wants everyone to know about His love. So He sent Jesus to be born.

She laid baby Jesus down in the manger. He slept where the animals eat. God's Son, Jesus, was born!

Shepherds and Angels

Luke 2:8-20

It was a quiet night. Stars twinkled high in the sky. Sheep and lambs lay sleeping together. Sleepy shepherds sat by their fire.

Suddenly, it was as bright as daytime! The shepherds looked up. An ANGEL! The angel said, "Don't be afraid! I have GOOD NEWS to tell everyone. In Bethlehem, JESUS, the Savior, is born! You'll find Him lying in a manger."

Then whole SKY turned bright. It was filled
with angels! The angels praised God and said,
"GLORY TO GOD IN THE HIGHEST!"

Then the angels were gone. It was very quiet and dark again. The shepherds looked at each other. They said, "Let's go to Bethlehem and see this BABY!" They hurried down the road!

The shepherds came to a stable. They could
see a newborn baby inside. He was lying in a
manger! They tiptoed in to see. Here was Jesus,
just as the angel had said! They were so happy!
They praised and thanked God.

When the shepherds left the stable, they told everyone they saw, "Listen! We have good news! Jesus is born! GOOD NEWS!"

Wise Men Worship Jesus

Matthew 2:1-15

Jesus was born! God placed a bright new star in
the sky. Far away, some wise men saw the star.
They knew a great new king was born! They
said, "Let's find this king. We'll bring gifts to
him!" So they loaded camels and began the trip.

They rode for days and days. One day, they reached Jerusalem. They went to King Herod's palace. They asked, "Where is the new King? We want to worship Him!"

King Herod wanted to be the ONLY king! Herod found out what God's Word said. It told where Jesus would be born. Herod told the wise men, "Go to Bethlehem. When you find the child, tell me so I can worship Him, too." But Herod really wanted to KILL Jesus!

The wise men followed the star to Bethlehem.
The star stopped over the place Jesus was!
The wise men got off their camels. They went
inside and bowed low. They gladly gave their
gifts. Here was Jesus, the King they had
followed the star to find!

The wise men MIGHT have gone back and told King Herod where Jesus was. But in a dream, God told them NOT to go back. They went home on a different road.

Then an angel told Joseph in a dream, "Get up! Take Mary and Jesus to Egypt. King Herod wants to hurt Jesus."

We can worship Jesus, too. We can give gifts of love and praise to Jesus.

Mary and Joseph picked up Jesus. They traveled quietly and quickly. After many days, they were in Egypt! God kept Joseph and Mary and Jesus safe!

Jesus at the Temple

Luke 2:41-52

Baby Jesus grew and grew! He grew taller and
stronger and wiser. Joseph was a carpenter. He
made things out of wood. He taught Jesus how
to make things, too.

When Jesus was 12 years old, His family traveled to Jerusalem. It was a holiday! They went to the Temple to worship. They sang and prayed to God. They visited with relatives and friends.

After a week, they started walking home.
Everyone was busy talking and walking. They
walked all day. No one noticed that JESUS
wasn't there!

But when everyone stopped to sleep, Mary and
Joseph looked for Jesus. They could not find
Him anywhere! WHERE could Jesus BE?

Mary and Joseph hurried back to Jerusalem.
They looked EVERYWHERE for Him. They
looked all over the city for three days! Then
they went to search the Temple. They stopped,
amazed! THERE was Jesus!

You are growing taller and stronger and wiser. God takes care of you as you grow.

Jesus was talking to the Temple leaders! He wasn't afraid or sad. He was there to talk about God, His Father. He knew God was taking care of Him!

John the Baptist

Matthew 3:1-17; Mark 1:1-11; Luke 3:1-22

John was Jesus' cousin. John lived alone out in the desert. He wore rough and simple clothes. He ate the food he found in the desert.

God had given John a special job. John told the
people, "Get ready! God will soon send the Savior!" John talked near the Jordan River. People
came from all the towns to listen!

John told people, "Stop doing wrong. Ask God to forgive you. Do what is right!"

The people asked, "What should we do?"

John said, "If you have two coats, give one to a person who has NO coat. If you have food, give some to HUNGRY people."

Some soldiers asked John, "What should WE do?"

John said, "Be honest. Don't take money that isn't yours. Be happy with what you have."

John baptized many people in the river. Being baptized showed a person wanted God to forgive the wrong things he or she did. One day, Jesus asked John to baptize HIM. John said, "YOU should baptize ME!" But Jesus said, "No. This is what God wants us to do. And I want to obey God."

So John baptized Jesus. Then God's Spirit, looking like a dove, came down from heaven to Jesus. God spoke from heaven. "This is My Son. I love Him. I am pleased with Him!"

Jesus Chooses Helpers

Matthew 4:18-22; Luke 5:27-28; 6:12-16; 9:1-6

Jesus walked by the Sea of Galilee. He saw
fishermen throwing big fishing nets out into
the water. Jesus called, "Peter! Andrew! Come,
follow Me. I'll teach you how to tell people about
God." The two men gladly went with Jesus!

Jesus walked on down the shore. He saw two other fishermen in a boat. "James and John!" Jesus called. "Come with Me!" James and John also went with Jesus. Now Jesus had FOUR helpers!

Later, Jesus saw a man named Matthew.
Matthew was working, collecting money.
"Follow Me, Matthew," said Jesus. Matthew
got right up and went with Jesus. Now Jesus
had FIVE friends to help Him!

We can be helpers for Jesus, too. We can talk about God's love.

Jesus asked more people to follow Him—six, seven, eight, nine, ten, eleven, twelve helpers! Jesus taught His 12 helpers many things about God's love. Jesus' helpers told other people what they'd learned about God's love!

Nicodemus and Jesus

John 3:1-17

Nicodemus was a leader in the big city of Jerusalem. Nicodemus wanted to know about Jesus.

One quiet night, Nicodemus came to see Jesus.
He said, "Jesus, we know You came from God.
No one else can do what You do!"

Jesus told Nicodemus that he needed to be born
again. Nicodemus didn't understand Jesus' words.
But Jesus explained that Nicodemus had to be
born into God's family.

God loves you! He wants you to believe in Jesus and be part of His family.

"God loves this world very much," Jesus said. "That's why He sent Me here. I am God's very own Son. When a person believes in Me, that person gets to be part of God's family now and forever!"

The Woman at the Well

John 4:3-42

Jesus and His helpers walked and walked. They walked until it was noon. They were hot, hungry and tired.

They stopped at a town to rest. Jesus' friends
went to buy food. Jesus sat by the well just
outside of the town.

A woman came to get water from the well.
Jesus asked her for a drink. She was surprised
Jesus would talk to her. Then Jesus surprised
her even more! He told about many things she
had done.

She was amazed. Jesus knew all about her! The woman said, "When the Savior comes, He'll talk to us like You are talking to me."

Jesus told her, "I AM the Savior God promised to send!"

The woman was VERY excited! She ran back into the town shouting, "Listen! There's a Man by the well. I think He's the SAVIOR God promised to send!"

Jesus knows what you are like and what you do. He loves you!

Many people came to meet Jesus for themselves! They listened to His words. They asked Him to tell them more about God's love! They told the woman, "You were right. Jesus IS the Savior God promised to send!"

A Sick Boy Is Made Well

John 4:46-53

A young boy was very, very sick! The boy's
father, a king's official, was afraid his son
might die. Then he heard this good news:
Jesus was not too far away!

The official HURRIED to where Jesus was.
"Please, Jesus!" he said. "Please come to my
house and make my son well! He might die!"

Jesus told the father, "You may go. Your son will live!" The official BELIEVED what Jesus said. So he turned around and started home!

While the official was still traveling home, his helpers came running to meet him. They were VERY excited! They said, "Sir! Sir! Your son is ALIVE. And he is WELL now!"

The official asked, "When did my boy get better?" They told him his son got better at the VERY time Jesus said he would live!

Jesus cares about you when you are sick. He can make you well.

The official, his son and their family believed in Jesus. He made a very sick boy well, just by SAYING SO!

Jesus Tells of God's Love

Matthew 6:25-34

Jesus sat on a hillside with His friends. Jesus knew that His friends worried about not having food to eat. Sometimes they worried about not having clothes to wear.

Jesus said, "Look at the birds in the sky! They don't worry. They don't tend gardens to grow food. Yet God makes sure they have food. God feeds birds. He will feed YOU, too!"

Then Jesus said, "Look at these flowers! They don't make clothes. But what a flower wears is more beautiful than a king's fanciest robe. GOD gives THEM beautiful clothes. God will give YOU clothes, too!"

Jesus will take care of us. He knows what you need every day.

Jesus said, "So don't worry. God knows what you need. God will take care of you!"

Friends Help a Lame Man

Mark 2:1-12

Four men had a friend who couldn't walk. He couldn't stand or run or skip! They KNEW Jesus could help their friend. The men wanted to take him to Jesus, but how could they GET him there?

The men laid their friend down on a mat. Each
man picked up a corner. The four men carried
and worked and walked together. They kept
walking until they got their friend to where
JESUS was!

At the house where Jesus was teaching, there were people EVERYWHERE! The men couldn't even get NEAR the door! How could they get their friend to Jesus?

The house had stairs up to the flat roof!
The men carried their friend up the stairs.
They broke and pulled and tore to make a big
HOLE in the ROOF! Then the four carefully
LOWERED their friend on his mat, right
through that hole!

Jesus watched the four men. He could see the
men KNEW He could heal their friend! He said
to the man on the mat, "Son, your sins are
forgiven. Get up, take your mat and go home."

Even when it's hard, we can help our friends.

The man got up. He picked up his mat and walked away! Now all FIVE friends could walk and run and skip back to their homes TOGETHER. Jesus had made their friend WELL!

Parable of the Sower

Matthew 13:3-23; Mark 4:3-20; Luke 8:5-15

Jesus told this story about a farmer who planted seeds. "Some seeds landed on hard dirt," Jesus said. "Birds ate up those seeds. This is like people who hear God's Word, but then quickly FORGET to obey it.

"Other seeds landed where there was only a little dirt. The seeds grew into baby plants. But the sun dried them out. This is like people who gladly hear God's Word but forget it when trouble comes.

"Other seeds landed in dirt where weeds were growing. The weeds CHOKED these plants. This is like people who start out obeying God's Word. But then they start to worry about all the things they want. They forget about God's care and help.

When we hear God's Word, we can do what it says.

"Some seeds landed on GOOD dirt. They grew into BIG plants! The big plants grew 100 times MORE than was planted! This is like people who hear and obey God's Word."

Jesus Stops a Storm

Matthew 8:23-27; Mark 4:1,35-41; Luke 8:22-25

Jesus had been teaching all day long. Now, the
sun was going down. Jesus said, "Let's go to the
other side." He and His friends got into a boat.
They began to sail across the big lake. Jesus lay
down in the boat and slept.

Suddenly, the wind began to blow HARD. The
wind made a BIG STORM! Waves splashed
high and wild! The waves filled the boat with
WATER. The boat was about to SINK!

Jesus' friends shouted at Jesus, "Jesus, WAKE UP! We're going to DROWN!"

Jesus got up and looked around. He said to the roaring wind and waves, "Quiet! Be still!" The wind died down. The waves were GONE. The lake was CALM!

Jesus looked at His friends. "Why are you so afraid?" He asked. "Don't you know you can trust Me?"

Jesus
is powerful.
He will take
care of us.

Jesus' friends were AMAZED! They looked at each other. They said to each other, "Even the WIND and WAVES obey Jesus!"

Jairus's Daughter

Matthew 9:18-26; Mark 5:21-43; Luke 8:40-56

A man named Jairus had a little girl. She was VERY sick, so sick she might die! Jairus found Jesus and knelt down. He said, "My little daughter is dying. Please come and put your hands on her so that she will be made well and live!"

As Jesus went with Jairus to his house, some
men stopped them. They said, "Jairus, don't
bother Jesus. Your daughter is dead."

Jesus looked at Jairus. "Don't be afraid," He
said. "Just believe."

Jesus and His friends came into the house.
People were crying because the girl had died.
Jesus said, "What is all this noise? The little
girl is asleep." The people at the house laughed
at Jesus.

Nothing is too hard for Jesus. He cares for you in good and bad times.

But Jesus went to the little girl's room and stood by her bed. Jesus took her by the hand. He said, "Little girl, get up!" And she DID! She got out of bed! She was ALIVE again! Her parents were happy and amazed. Jesus made a dead girl LIVE!

Jesus Feeds 5,000

Mark 6:30-44; John 6:1-13

A big crowd of people listened to Jesus talk about God. They listened all day! They got very HUNGRY!

Jesus' friends said, "Let's send these hungry people home. They need to eat." Jesus asked, "Why don't YOU give them food?"

His friends said, "That would take LOTS of money and there is no place to even buy food!"

Jesus' friend Andrew brought a little boy to Jesus. He said, "Jesus, this little boy has five little loaves of bread. He has two little fishes. How can such a little lunch feed so MANY hungry people?"

The little boy gave Jesus his lunch. Jesus
smiled and said, "Thank you!"

Then Jesus said, "Have everyone sit on the grass." He thanked God for the little lunch. Jesus gave pieces of bread and fish to His friends.

Jesus loves us so much He helps us have the things we need.

Jesus' friends gave food to each girl, boy, woman and man! The food did NOT get used up! There was plenty for everyone.

Jesus told His friends to gather up the leftovers. They gathered up TWELVE baskets of food! Jesus had made enough food—and MORE besides!

Jesus Heals a Blind Man

John 9:1-11,35-38

Jesus and His friends saw a blind man. He could not see or work or play. Jesus' friends asked, "Jesus, why is this man blind? Did he do something wrong?"

Jesus said, "No. God is about to do something wonderful in his life."

Then Jesus spit on the ground. He made some mud from the dust. He put the mud on the man's eyes!

Jesus said to the man, "Go, walk to the pool of water called Siloam. Wash the mud away." So the man went, feeling his way along.

He got to the pool. He washed off the mud. Do
you know what happened? He could SEE!

Everyone who saw the man was AMAZED! "You look like the blind man who used to sit right here!" they said.

"YES!" he said. "I'm the same man! Jesus made my eyes to SEE!"

Jesus loves us. He wants to help us in wonderful ways.

Later, Jesus found the man. He said, "Do you believe in Me?"

The man knew Jesus' voice. Here was the One who had made his eyes to see! The man said, "Lord, I BELIEVE!"

The Greatest of All

Mark 9:33-37; Luke 9:46-48

Jesus' friends were walking along, arguing.
They argued about who was IMPORTANT.
They argued about who was GREATEST.

When they came indoors Jesus asked, "What were you arguing about on the road?" No one wanted to tell Jesus. But Jesus KNEW what they'd been saying.

Jesus called His friends to come and sit with Him. Jesus said, "Do you want GOD to think you're IMPORTANT?" Jesus asked. "Then treat everyone else like they are MORE important than YOU are!"

He pulled a little child close to Him. Jesus said, "When you are kind to a child, it is the same as being kind to Me. When you welcome a child, it is the same as being glad to see Me."

When we are kind and helpful, God thinks we are the best!

The Forgiving King

Matthew 18:21-35

This is a story Jesus told: A king's helper owed money to the king. The king said, "PAY me what you owe!" The helper did NOT have money to pay! So he begged the king to wait. The king was kind. He said, "I forgive you. You don't have to pay ANY money back!"

The helper was VERY GLAD to be forgiven! But on his way home, he saw a friend. This friend owed him a LITTLE money. He grabbed him and said, "PAY ME NOW!"

The friend said, "Please wait! I will pay!" But the king's helper put his friend in JAIL!

When others are mean to us, we are sad. God will help us forgive and be kind.

The king heard about his mean helper. He called the helper in and said, "I forgave you a LOT of money. You should have been kind to your friend like I was kind to you!" So the king put the helper in jail because he did not show kindness and forgive.

The Good Samaritan

Luke 10:25-37

A man was walking a long way. While he walked, some men grabbed him, hurt him and took all his money. The man lay hurting on the ground. He couldn't even get up!

But soon, an important leader walked by! The hurt man lay there, waiting for help. But the leader DIDN'T help! He hurried away!

The hurt man groaned. He hurt all OVER! But
now ANOTHER man came near. He stopped
and LOOKED at the hurt man. The hurt man
lay there, waiting for help. But the second man
hurried away, too!

The hurt man could only lie on the ground. But then he heard a clippety-clop sound. A donkey stopped. Another man got off. THIS man put medicine on the man's sores. He bandaged the man's cuts.

God loves everyone! He wants us to show His love and be kind to others.

He put the hurt man on the donkey and brought him to a safe place. He paid money to be sure that the hurt man would be taken care of. The man on the donkey SHOWED God's love. He was kind to the hurt man!

Jesus Teaches on Prayer

Luke 11:1-13

Jesus often went away quietly to pray to God, His Father. One day, Jesus' friends saw Him praying. They said, "Lord, teach US to pray!"

Jesus said, "When you pray, pray like this: 'Our Father in heaven, we love and respect Your name. We want You to be King over us always. Give us what we need for this day.

'Forgive the wrong things we do. We forgive
people who did wrong to us. Please protect us
from doing wrong. Help us to do right. Amen.'"

Jesus said, "Ask God for what you need. Be brave. Don't give up. You knock on a door until it opens! So in the same way, keep on asking God. Expect Him to answer!

We can talk to God. He hears us when we pray.

"If your child asked you for bread, would you give your child a rock instead? Of course not! You give good things to your children. And remember, God is YOUR Father. He is the very BEST Father! He loves you and wants to give you what is best!"

The Lost Sheep

Luke 15:3-7

Jesus told a story about a shepherd who took good care of his sheep. This shepherd had 100 sheep.

One sheep got lost! So the shepherd looked and looked for the lost sheep. He called the sheep's name! He finally found the sheep and brought it home.

God loves you! When you believe in Jesus, God is glad.

The shepherd was so GLAD he had found the sheep. He had a party with his friends. Jesus said that God loves us like a good shepherd. When we become part of God's family, God celebrates!

The Loving Father

Luke 15:11-24

Jesus told a story about a farmer who had two sons. The younger son said, "Father, give me my share of the money from our farm." So his father gave him a lot of money.

The younger son soon left home. He made new friends and had big parties. He spent lots of money!

But one day, his money was all GONE! He did
not have ANY food! So the son had to get a job.
He worked in a muddy pig pen, feeding the pigs.
But he was still VERY hungry!

He said, "I'm SO hungry I could eat the PIGS'
food! I'm really sorry I left home. Even my
father's servants have plenty to eat! I'm
going HOME. I'll ask my father to make me
his SERVANT!"

The son walked and walked toward home.
When he was still far down the road, his father
saw him coming. His father RAN to him. He
was GLAD to see his son! He hugged his son
and kissed him!

God is like a loving dad. God never stops loving you!

The father gave his son new clothes. He put a ring on his hand and new shoes on his feet. Then he had a big party to celebrate because his son had come home!

One Man Thanks Jesus

Luke 17:11-19

Ten men stood beside the road. They were sick with leprosy. This meant that they could not be around other people. They couldn't live with their families.

But the 10 sick men saw JESUS coming down the road! They knew Jesus made sick people WELL. So the 10 sick men called to Jesus, "Jesus! MASTER! Please HELP us!"

Jesus stopped and looked at the men. He said,
"Go. Show yourselves to the priests so you can
prove you are well."

WOW! The men began to RUN. And as they ran, they could SEE that they were not sick anymore. They were WELL!

Nine men ran and ran, happy to go home to their families! But one of the men STOPPED.

Jesus helps us every day. Remember to thank Him!

He turned around and RAN back to Jesus. He bowed down at Jesus' feet. He THANKED Jesus for making him well!

Jesus Loves Children

Matthew 19:13-15; Mark 10:13-16

Some families were going to see Jesus. The parents wanted Jesus to pray for their children.

The families walked and walked. Parents carried tired little ones. No one wanted to stop! When they saw a crowd of people, they asked, "Is Jesus here?" He was!

The families hurried to where Jesus was!
But as they got close to Jesus, Jesus' friends
stepped in their way. The men said, "STOP!
Don't bother Jesus. He is too BUSY to see
children. Go away!"

The children and parents were sad. Slowly, they
turned to leave.

But Jesus saw what was happening. Jesus was NOT happy! He said to His friends, "Let the children COME to Me! NEVER tell them to go away. God's Kingdom belongs to ones like these!"

Jesus loves you. He wants to be your friend.

Then Jesus motioned for the children. They ran to Him! He took them in His arms and held them. He prayed for them. Jesus was NOT too busy for the children. He didn't want them to go away! Jesus LOVES children!

399

A Rich Man's Question

Matthew 19:16-26; Mark 10:17-27; Luke 18:18-27

A rich young man knelt in front of Jesus. He asked, "Good Teacher, what should I DO so that I can live forever?"

Jesus said, "Do what God says. Obey Him!"

The young man said, "I have DONE that since I was just a boy!"

Jesus said, "Then do this: Sell everything you have and give all your money to poor people. Then come and follow Me." The young man did NOT want to do that! He sadly walked away.

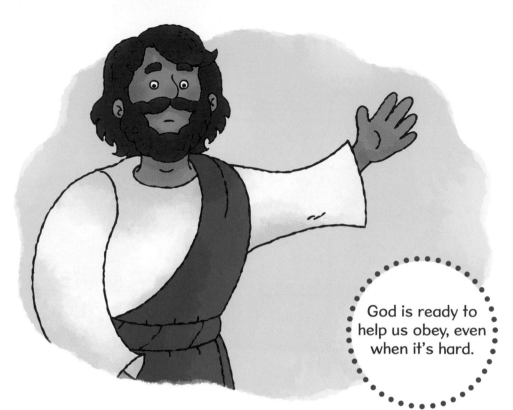

God is ready to help us obey, even when it's hard.

Jesus told His friends, "People who love money have a hard time loving God." Jesus' friends asked, "Then who CAN be saved and have life that lasts forever?"

"NO person can do it alone," said Jesus. "But God CAN do anything! Nothing is too hard for Him."

Jesus Loves Zacchaeus

Luke 19:1-10

Zacchaeus was a tax collector. People did NOT like him much. He took more money than was fair. And taking that money made him RICH.

Zacchaeus heard that Jesus was coming. He wanted to SEE Jesus! But Zacchaeus was very short. He could NEVER see over all the people in a crowd.

So Zacchaeus ran AHEAD of the crowd. He climbed up into a tree! Now he was taller than ANYONE!

When Jesus walked right under that tree, He STOPPED. He looked up, right at Zacchaeus! He said, "Zacchaeus, please come down. I must stay at your house today!"

Zacchaeus hurried down the tree. WOW! Jesus was coming to HIS house! The people in the crowd grumbled, "Zacchaeus is such a bad man. Why is Jesus going with HIM?"

We can say we're sorry when we do wrong. Jesus will forgive us and help us do right.

Zacchaeus looked at Jesus. He wanted to show he had CHANGED! He said, "Look, Lord! Here and now, I give half of what I own to poor people. And if I have cheated anyone, I will pay them back FOUR TIMES what I took!"

Jesus said, "Today God's salvation has come to Zacchaeus's house!"

Palm Sunday

Matthew 21:1-11,15-16; Mark 11:1-10; Luke 19:28-38

Jesus and His friends were walking. Jesus told two friends, "Go into the village ahead. You'll find a donkey tied there. Untie it and bring it to Me." Jesus' friends found the donkey. They led it to Jesus and laid their coats across the donkey's back.

Jesus got on the donkey. He began riding
toward Jerusalem. Many OTHER people were
going to Jerusalem, too! These people were glad
to see Jesus. They shouted praises to Jesus!

Some people cut tree branches and laid them on the road. Other people laid their coats on the road. They made the road look like a colorful carpet for Jesus' donkey to walk upon! This was the way people welcomed a king!

All around Jesus, people waved branches. They sang and shouted praises to Jesus. It looked like a big parade made just to welcome Jesus into Jerusalem!

Jesus rode the donkey through Jerusalem.
At the Temple, He got off the donkey. Many
children were with Him, singing and shouting
their praises to Jesus!

Because we're happy that Jesus is God's Son, we can sing praise to Him!

Some of the leaders did not like what the children were singing and shouting. They said, "Do you HEAR what those children are SAYING?" Jesus said, "Yes! God has brought praise from the lips of children!" Jesus was GLAD to hear the children!

The Poor Woman's Gift

Mark 12:41-44; Luke 21:1-4

Jesus sat near the doors of the Temple. He watched the people walk in. They threw their money offerings into the big offering boxes.

Some people threw in lots of money. Their many coins made a loud clang clang! Other people gave only a little money. Their few coins made a chink chink! But they all still had much more money at home.

Then a woman walked in. She brought two
small coins. They were worth less than a penny!
It was all the money she had. She wanted to
show God she loved Him. She put her two coins
into the offering box. The two tiny coins made a
tiny tink tink!

We show love for God when we share what we have with others.

Jesus said to His friends, "Did you see that woman? She gave more than the richest people! They all still have lots of money left at home. But those two little coins were all she had. She gave it ALL to God to show her love!"

Jesus' Last Supper

Matthew 26:17-30; Mark 14:12-26; Luke 22:7-20; John 13:1-17

Jesus was in Jerusalem with His friends. It was
a special time of year called Passover*. Jesus
asked His friends to make a special meal. Soon
Jesus and His friends came to the meal. Jesus
washed the feet of His friends. "I have done this
to teach you to serve and help each other,"
Jesus said.

* Passover is a week-long holiday when God's people remember how He helped
  them escape from slavery in Egypt.

419

Then Jesus and His friends ate the special
Passover meal together. After the meal, Jesus
broke bread into pieces. He gave a piece to each
of His friends and said, "This is My body." He
did this to show them that His body would soon
be broken for them.

Jesus loves us so much! He wants us to love each other, too.

Then Jesus passed around a cup. He said, "Drink from it, all of you. This is My blood that shows God's promise to save you." Jesus said these words because He knew He would die soon.

Jesus in Gethsemane

Matthew 26:36-50; Mark 14:32-46; Luke 22:39-48; John 18:1-9

Jesus and His friends ate their Passover meal.
They sang a song together. Then they walked
up a hill to a place called Gethsemane. On the
hill, Jesus went to pray by Himself. He prayed
alone for a long time. He asked God, His Father,
to do what was best.

A little later, Jesus' friend Judas found Jesus. He greeted Jesus, "Hello, Rabbi!" But Judas was not alone. He had brought a crowd of angry men. They had torches and swords and sticks.

Jesus trusted God to do good things, even when people did bad things to Him.

These men took Jesus and led Him away. Jesus' friends were afraid. They wondered, *What will happen to Jesus?*

Jesus Dies and Lives Again

Matthew 26:58-68; 27:11—28:10; Mark 14:53—16:10; Luke 22:63—24:9;
John 18:1—20:20

Jesus let angry people take Him away. He
listened while they told lies about Him. He
let them hurt Him.

Then Jesus let them kill Him on a cross. Jesus'
friends were very sad and scared.

Jesus' friends put His body into a tomb. A tomb is like a little cave in a hill. Soldiers rolled a HUGE stone over the door. The men who killed Jesus wanted to make sure that no one could get into His tomb!

But three days later, Mary came to the tomb. That HUGE stone had been moved! So she looked inside the tomb. There were two ANGELS in the tomb! One angel asked, "Why are you crying?"

Mary said, "I don't know where Jesus is!" The angel said, "He is not here. He has risen, just as He said!"

Mary turned and left the tomb. Oops! She almost bumped into someone. "Mary!" a voice said. Mary knew that voice. It was Jesus' voice! Jesus was ALIVE! He was standing right there in front of her!

Jesus did not stay dead. He is alive and He loves us!

Jesus told Mary, "Go and tell the others."
Mary was GLAD. She ran to tell Jesus' other
friends! "Jesus is ALIVE!" she said. "I SAW
Him!" Some of Jesus' friends didn't believe her
at first. But they ran to the tomb. It was empty!
Soon, they saw Jesus, too. Then they knew:
Jesus is ALIVE!

Thomas Sees Jesus

John 20:19-31

After Jesus was ALIVE again, He came to the
room where His friends were. When they saw
Jesus, they were very glad!

But Thomas had been gone when Jesus came!
Thomas's friends told him, "We've seen JESUS.
He is not dead. He is ALIVE!"

But Thomas said, "I don't believe you. Unless I
touch Him, I won't believe you!"

Seven days later, Jesus came to visit again.
This time, Thomas was there! The doors were
locked. But that did not stop Jesus. He walked
right into the room! Thomas stared. He could
SEE that it was Jesus!

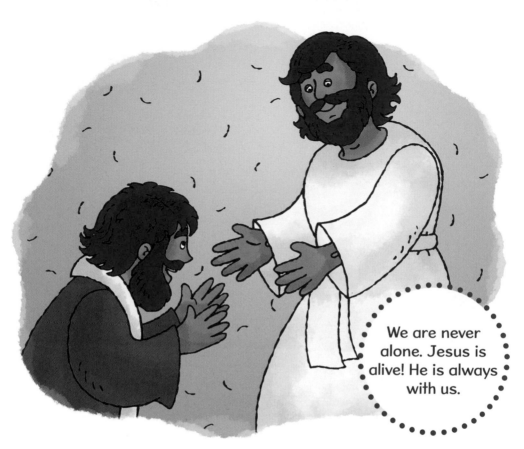

We are never alone. Jesus is alive! He is always with us.

Jesus said to Thomas, "LOOK at My hands. TOUCH My side. Then BELIEVE!" Thomas bowed down at Jesus' feet. "My Lord and God!" he said. Now Thomas knew Jesus was not dead. And the same good news STILL is true: JESUS IS ALIVE!

Breakfast on the Beach

John 21:1-17

Jesus was alive again! His friends had seen Him two times now. One evening Peter said, "I'm going fishing." He and his friends went out in a boat at night.

All night long, they threw out their big nets and then pulled the nets back in. But there were NO fish! They did this all night. Still NO fish! The sun began to rise. Peter could see someone on the shore. The man called out, "Did you catch any fish?" "NO!" Peter shouted back.

The man said, "Throw out your net on the right side of the boat. You'll find some." The men did. And the nets FILLED with fish! Suddenly John said to Peter, "It's JESUS!"

Peter JUMPED out of the boat and SWAM! He
wanted to get to JESUS! Everyone else rowed the
boats to shore, dragging the heavy nets full of
fish. When they got to the shore, Jesus had fish
and bread already cooked for them to eat.

Later, Jesus talked to Peter. Before Jesus died, Peter had told people that he did not know Jesus. He even said he'd never MET Jesus. Peter had been VERY sorry for his words. Jesus wanted Peter to know he was forgiven.

Jesus never stops loving us, even when we do wrong. He will help us obey.

Jesus told Peter about His good plan for him. Jesus told Peter, "Be like a shepherd. Help people learn about Me and follow Me." He told Peter this three times. Jesus still loved Peter.

The Ascension

Matthew 28:16-20; Acts 1:3-11

Jesus visited His friends for 40 more days. Jesus told them, "Wait in Jerusalem." He promised to send the Holy Spirit to help them.

When it was time for Jesus to return to heaven, He walked with His friends to a mountain. On that mountain, Jesus told His friends, "Remember, I am always with you. After I have gone back to heaven, tell people everywhere the good news that I love them. Help them believe in Me and obey the things I taught you."

Then Jesus began to rise up into the sky! His friends were surprised! Jesus went UP and UP until He was in a cloud. His friends couldn't see Jesus anymore.

Suddenly two ANGELS were there! The angels said, "Why are you standing here looking into the sky? Jesus will come back someday, just as you saw Him go!"

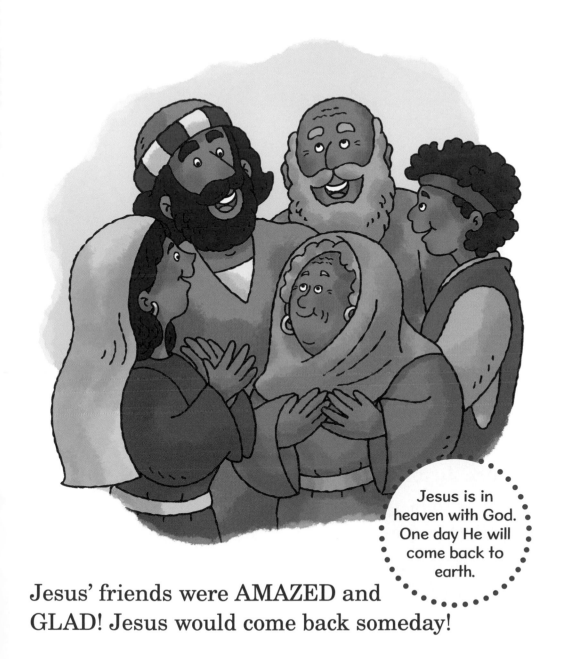

Jesus is in heaven with God. One day He will come back to earth.

Jesus' friends were AMAZED and GLAD! Jesus would come back someday!

Pentecost

Acts 1:1-5,12-14; 2:1-41

Before Jesus went back to heaven, He told His friends to stay in Jerusalem. "Wait for the gift My Father promised you," Jesus said. "He will send the Holy Spirit. The Holy Spirit will give you power to tell people EVERYWHERE about Me!"

Jesus' friends stayed together in Jerusalem. They prayed and waited. One day, they heard a sound like wind blowing. They looked at each other. Little FLAMES were burning over their heads! When they spoke, other languages came out!

Everyone was SO excited that they ran outside!
As they ran out, a huge crowd of people came
running toward them! So Jesus' friends began
telling wonderful things about God! In the
crowd were people who spoke many different
languages. But the Holy Spirit made the words
clear in EVERY language!

Then Jesus' friend Peter stood up. He told how Jesus lived and died and came back to life so that people could join God's family. That day, more and more people loved Jesus! God's family grew bigger and BIGGER.

A Lame Man Walks

Acts 3:1-16

There was a man who could not walk or run. He was born that way. He couldn't work or play or help his friends. Every day, he lay on a mat by the Temple gate. He asked people for money.

One day, Peter and John walked by this man.
He asked for money, as he always did. Peter
said, "Look at us." The man looked up. Peter
said, "I do NOT have money to give you. But
I'll give you what I DO have. In the name of
Jesus, WALK!" Peter took the man by the hand.

The man's legs were STRONG! He stood! He could tiptoe and march. He could skip and he could jump! He walked and leaped and bounced and danced into the Temple behind Peter and John!

Jesus has the power to make sick people well. We can praise Him!

EVERYONE knew this man! He had sat by the Temple gate for YEARS. Peter told the people how God had healed the man in Jesus' name. He told them all about Jesus while they watched the man show how his legs could leap and walk!

Barnabas Shares

Acts 4:32-37

God's family was glad to share the things they had! No one said, "This is MINE. You can't have any!" Instead, people said, "Would you like some? There is PLENTY for both of us!"

If people needed food, other people gave them
the food they needed. If people needed clothes,
other people brought them the clothes they
needed.

People who owned houses or fields sold them.
They brought the money they made to the
leaders of God's family. The leaders used it
to help EVERYONE.

Sharing with others helps them and is a good way to tell God we love Him.

One man named Barnabas sold his field. He didn't keep his money for himself. He was GLAD to share what he had. In God's family, no one needed ANYTHING because everyone shared EVERYTHING!

Food for Widows

Acts 6:1-7

God's family was growing! But there was a problem. Some women weren't getting enough to eat. They were still hungry! They felt forgotten. Jesus' friends wanted God's family to have more LOVE, not more hunger!

Jesus' friends knew they needed to keep on
telling people about Jesus. They couldn't solve
this problem themselves. So they asked everyone to choose some helpers. These helpers would
work to make sure everyone got enough food.

They chose one, two, three, four helpers. But they needed to be sure they had enough! So they chose one, two, three more. The problem was solved! The seven men helped EVERYONE in God's family to have the food they needed!

Philip and the Ethiopian Leader

Acts 8:26-40

Philip loved God. One day an angel came with a job for Philip. The angel said, "Go and walk on the road that leads toward the town of Gaza."

God had a job for Philip, and he obeyed! Philip began to walk down that road. Soon, he heard the sound of horses' hooves. A chariot was coming, a cart to ride in. It was pulled by horses!

Inside the chariot, a man was reading. The man was a leader from a faraway country. He was reading a scroll of God's Word. God told Philip, "Run up to the chariot."

Philip RAN! He got close to the chariot. When Philip saw what the leader was reading, he asked, "Do you understand these words?"

"No! I need someone to help me!" the man said.

The leader invited Philip to sit with him. Philip
climbed into the chariot. Together, they read
the words on the scroll. The words were about
Jesus! So Philip started telling him about Jesus!

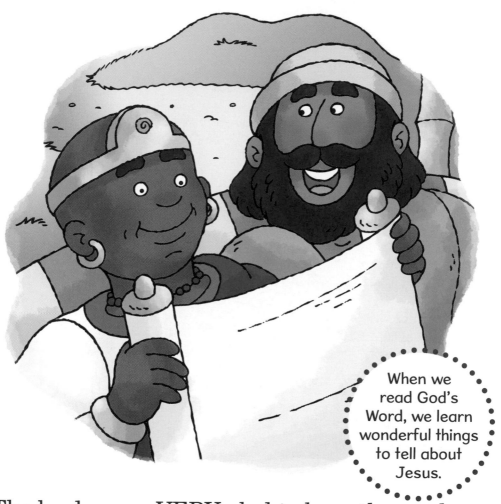

When we read God's Word, we learn wonderful things to tell about Jesus.

The leader was VERY glad to hear the good news that Jesus loved him! He believed Jesus is God's Son. He joined God's family, right there on the road!

Paul Meets Jesus

Acts 9:1-20

Many people were learning about Jesus. They loved Jesus! But a man named Paul* did NOT believe that Jesus is God's Son. He wanted to STOP people who loved Jesus.

* At this time, Paul's name was Saul. But later, he became known as Paul.

Paul was going to the big city of Damascus. He was going there to find people who loved Jesus. He would put them in jail! When Paul and his friends were almost to Damascus, a bright light shone! Paul fell to the ground. He couldn't SEE!

Then Paul heard a voice. It was Jesus! "Why are you hurting Me?" Jesus asked. Hurting Jesus' friends hurt Jesus, too! Paul was surprised! He asked Jesus what to do. Jesus said, "Go into the city. Wait there."

Paul waited for three days. He didn't eat any food. He prayed and prayed.

God told a man named Ananias to visit Paul. At first, Ananias was afraid. He knew that Paul had come to Damascus to hurt Jesus' friends! But God told Ananias it would be all right. So Ananias came and prayed for Paul. Paul's eyes were well. He could SEE again!

God wants everyone to love Him and be part of His family.

Now Paul LOVED Jesus! He began telling people that Jesus is God's Son! He had come to Damascus planning to hurt Jesus' friends. But now Paul was one of Jesus' friends!

Paul Escapes

Acts 9:20-28

Paul was Jesus' friend! He was telling people in Damascus about Jesus. Some people were NOT glad about this. Paul's words about Jesus made them angry. They said, "We must STOP Paul. We will catch him and kill him!"

These men made a plan. Damascus had a high
wall all around it. The ONLY way out of it was
through the gates. The men agreed, "We will
watch the gates day and night. We'll watch and
wait and catch PAUL!"

But Paul's friends found out about the plan. They said, "We can't let them hurt Paul!" So Paul's friends made a plan to help him. They got a great BIG basket and a very strong, very LONG rope.

At nighttime, Paul's friends took him to a high window in the city wall. Paul got into the big basket. His friends tied the long rope firmly to it. Then they slid the basket out the window. They let it down and down OUTSIDE the wall!

We can be ready to help our friends. This shows we love God.

It might have been a little bumpy and scary! But Paul knew God was with him. Finally, the basket landed with a THUMP! Paul was safe!

Peter Helps Dorcas

Acts 9:36-43

Dorcas was a very kind lady. She loved to sew and make clothes for people. She often gave the clothes she made to poor people who needed clothes. They were glad for the warm coats she made!

One day Dorcas got very sick and DIED! Dorcas's friends were SO sad. What could they do? They heard that Peter was in a town nearby. Two of Dorcas's friends hurried to get Peter! Peter came right back with the men.

Peter met Dorcas's sad, crying friends. They showed him clothes Dorcas had made. Then Peter asked Dorcas's friends to leave. Peter prayed to God. Then he said, "Dorcas, get up!" Dorcas opened her eyes. She sat up. And she GOT UP!

Dorcas's friends came back into the room. There
was Dorcas—ALIVE! Everyone KNEW Dorcas
had been dead. Dorcas's friends were very glad!

Peter Escapes from Prison

Acts 12:1-18

Peter was put into prison by the king. His friends were afraid he'd be killed! What could they do to help him? They could PRAY. So they prayed, day and night!

Peter was chained between two guards. Many more soldiers guarded the prison. But God sent an angel! The angel said, "Get up, Peter, and follow me!" The chains fell off Peter's hands. But both guards stayed ASLEEP!

Peter followed the angel through the prison. Not ONE guard woke up. The big prison gate swung open by itself. Peter thought he was dreaming! The angel led him a little way and then left. Peter was standing in the street. He was FREE!

Peter said to himself, "GOD has rescued me!"
So he hurried to where his friends were pray-
ing. He knocked on the door and a girl named
Rhoda answered. Peter said, "It's me! Peter!
I'm out of prison!"

Rhoda was so GLAD Peter was safe that she forgot to open the door! Instead, she ran to tell everyone who had been praying, "PETER is here!" They didn't believe her at first. But she kept saying, "No, it's really PETER!"

God takes care of our friends and us in scary times. He never leaves us alone.

Peter waited and waited. Finally, the door opened! Peter came inside. He told his friends how GOD had rescued him! They were GLAD to see Peter. And they were VERY glad to hear and see what GOD had done to answer their prayers!

Paul Tells about Jesus

Acts 16:9-15

Paul went MANY places to tell people the good news about Jesus! One night, Paul had a dream. In his dream a man said to Paul, "Come to my country and help us!"

In the morning, Paul and his friends agreed: God wanted them to travel to that country and tell the people there about Jesus. So they got right onto a big ship! The ship sailed for days and days. They got to the country, called Macedonia. They stayed in Philippi, the main city.

Soon, Paul and his friends walked outside the
city to where the river flowed. People often
came there to pray. Paul and his friends saw
a group of women who were there praying
together.

Paul began to tell these women the good news about Jesus! One lady there was named Lydia. She had her own business, selling purple cloth. Lydia heard what Paul said about Jesus. She believed in Jesus and joined God's family!

Lydia asked Paul and his friends, "Please come and stay at my house." So they went to Lydia's home. She kindly gave them food to eat. She gave them a safe place to sleep. That way, Paul and his friends could tell even MORE people about Jesus!

Singing in Jail

Acts 16:16-34

Paul and Silas were in Philippi. They were telling many people about Jesus! They helped a slave girl get well. But this made the girl's owners very ANGRY. The angry men grabbed Paul and Silas. They took them to the city officials!

The city officials had Paul and Silas BEATEN. Then they had them put into the JAIL. Their feet were locked between blocks of wood. Their bodies hurt all over! But Paul and Silas knew God cared about them.

So Paul and Silas began to pray. They began to
sing! They sang songs of praise and thanks to
God. Everyone in the jail could hear them
singing!

At midnight, the GROUND began to shake! It shook harder and HARDER! The doors to the jail cells popped open! The locks broke! The chains fell off! All the prisoners could run away!

The jailer RAN into the jail! He was afraid his prisoners were gone. But Paul called, "Don't worry! We're all here!"

The jailer was thankful. He asked, "What must I do to be saved?" Paul and Silas said, "Believe in the Lord Jesus Christ. You will be saved!"

In every situation, we can be glad and thankful to God for His love.

The jailer believed. He was filled with JOY! Then his whole FAMILY believed in Jesus! The jailer took care of Paul and Silas's sores. His family made a big meal for them. The next day, Paul and Silas went to another city to tell more people about Jesus!

Paul Obeys God

Acts 21:17—22

Paul came to Jerusalem. He wanted to tell Jesus' friends there about the MANY people all over who now loved Jesus! Jesus' friends were glad to hear this!

One day, Paul went to the Temple to pray. Some people saw Paul there. They were ANGRY that Paul loved Jesus. They shouted, "There is Paul! He teaches people to disobey our rules!" They dragged Paul out of the Temple. Soon, an angry crowd was around Paul!

Because of the noise, some soldiers came. They thought Paul had done something wrong! So they put chains on Paul. They asked, "Who is he? What did he do?" The soldiers couldn't understand what the angry crowd was shouting!

Then Paul asked, "May I talk to these people?"
The leader said yes. When the people became
quiet, Paul said, "I used to hurt people who
loved Jesus. But now I love Jesus, too. God has
told me to tell EVERYONE the good news that
Jesus is God's Son. And I must obey God!"

Paul's Nephew Helps

Acts 23:12-35

Paul was in jail even though he had not done anything wrong. And now, 40 angry men had agreed: "We will not eat or drink until Paul is DEAD." These 40 men made a plan to trick the soldiers. When the soldiers brought Paul out of the jail, the 40 men would GRAB him!

But Paul's nephew heard about the awful plan.
So he went to visit his Uncle Paul in jail. He
told Paul ALL about the plan! Paul sent him to
the commander of the soldiers.

Paul's nephew told the commander about the plan those men made. Their plan was to kill Paul. But the commander had a plan, too! He had a plan to keep Paul safe.

God wants us to always be ready to help others in big and little ways.

That night, the commander put Paul on a horse.
Around Paul, he put 70 soldiers on horses.
Around the horses walked 400 MORE soldiers.
The soldiers walked right through the city gate.
The 40 men looking for Paul never SAW him.
Paul was safe!

Safe in a Shipwreck

Acts 27

Paul and his friends were on a big ship. They were sailing far across the water to the big city of Rome. It was the stormy time of year!

They sailed on, hoping to escape the storms.
But one day, the sky filled with dark clouds.
Rain poured and strong winds blew the ship!
The waves splashed higher and HIGHER. The
waves threw the ship UP and DOWN. The
water WHOOSHED into the ship!

For days, the storm kept on blowing! The people on the ship were afraid. They thought they were going to die! But Paul said, "Don't be afraid. God sent an angel to tell me that God will keep us safe. The ship will break up, but we'll be safe on an island!"

The storm kept up for two more WEEKS!
Finally, the sailors could tell the ship was
getting near land. Paul gave the people bread
and told them to eat. They needed to be strong
and ready.

Then the strong waves CRASHED! The ship
began to break apart. The people jumped into
the water and grabbed floating pieces of wood.

When we have hard times, we can remember God's love and care. We can tell our friends, too!

The people floated to a little island. God kept them safe, just as He promised.

God's Family Grows

Acts 28—Jude 25

On the island of Malta, Paul and his friends told people about Jesus. Later, they sailed on another ship to Rome. In Rome, Paul told MORE people about Jesus!

As more people joined God's family, they kept
on telling people THEY knew about Jesus! All
of these people needed to know how to LIVE
and grow up in God's family.

So Jesus' friends wrote letters to God's family!
When a letter came from one of Jesus' friends,
God's family read that letter over and over again.

Paul wrote MANY letters to God's family.
He helped them know more about Jesus.
His letters taught ways to love and obey
God. Jesus' friends James, Peter and John
also wrote letters to God's family.

God has a big family. Everyone who loves His Son, Jesus, is part of God's family.

As the message of God's love spread all around the world, God's family grew and grew!

The Never-Ending Story

Revelation 1; 21—22

John was one of Jesus' closest friends. He told
people everywhere about Jesus! To stop John
from telling about Jesus, the king put John on
an island by himself. But while John was on
this island, Jesus showed him AMAZING things
that will happen.

Jesus showed John that God will finally bring an end to everything that's bad. No one will ever be sick or sad or tired or old! Jesus showed John what heaven would be like. Everyone will be full of joy and laughter. God's family will sing and praise God.

Jesus also showed John that heaven has gates made of big pearls. The city has walls and streets of pure gold. Heaven has plenty of room for everyone in God's family! And it will last FOREVER.

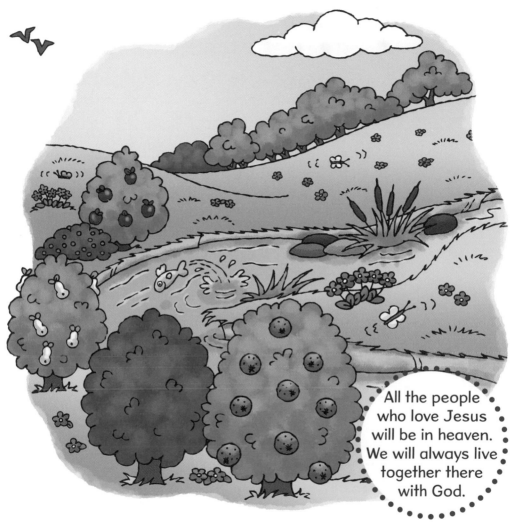

All the people who love Jesus will be in heaven. We will always live together there with God.

In heaven, it will never be night. Trees will grow with fruit all of the time. It will be the most amazing place EVER!

Gospel Light

The *God's Story for Me Bible Storybook*
contains the same Bible stories used in
Gospel Light's Preschool Sunday School Curriculum.
It is a wonderful resource for teachers to use in the
classroom *and* for parents to use at home, to
reinforce the stories children hear at church.

But there's lots more where this comes from!
To find out more about Gospel Light's creative Bible
teaching resources for parents *and* teachers, please
contact your local Christian bookstore or visit
www.gospellight.com

Use these fun stickers to personalize your Bible storybook. The stickers can show your favorite story, a story you read on your birthday, a picture that reminds you that God loves you, or a story you want to read again and again! Where will YOU put your stickers?

My favorite story!

Cool animals!

I love Jesus!

I prayed tonight!

Thank you, God!

Good story!

Please read this one again!

I like this story!

I heard this in Sunday School.

That's amazing!

Jesus is risen! Easter Sunday

I love God!